BETTER
COUNTRY WINES

BETTER COUNTRY WINES

P. W. TOMBS

AMATEUR WINEMAKER

Amateur Winemaker Publications

Published by
Argus Books Limited
1 Golden Square
London W1R 3AB

© Argus Books Limited 1985

ISBN 0 900841 79 6

Typeset by Sprint Ltd.
Printed in Great Britain by
Standard Press (Anodover) Ltd.

4

CONTENTS

INTRODUCTION

Selective Winemaking

The aims of this book are simple. There are excellent works on basic winemaking, but the next stage available seems to be a sudden leap to a complicated, scientific approach. This book sets out to take the winemaker on from a basic understanding of the hobby to the use of only sound ingredients. It will reduce disappointments to a minimum and explain how you can build up a cellar of excellent traditional wines and then move on to creating your own recipes.

I have taken the bull by the horns. Whole categories of wines which grandmother used to make need deleting from the recipe books. They need putting aside as inferior or unreliable. Authors just do not seem to qualify wines by reference to their quality.

In moving to selective winemaking I have tried not to overlook the beginner. All the basics of equipment and method are covered, so that a newcomer can start on the right footing.

Traditional wines are categorised in order of quality: the First Division, the Second Division and those which we can relegate to the lower divisions. Emphasis is placed upon the benefits of mixing ingredients to produce balanced and interesting wines. Modern ingredients (those which we can buy all year round from supermarkets or multiple stores) are introduced, examined and incorporated into more traditional recipes. Armed with all these available products and fruits the winemaker is pointed towards the surprisingly easy way of creating his own recipes.

The truth is that a lot of home winemaking is still a waste of time. The standpoint of authors on the subject has been either to attempt to imitate the grape, at the expense of any resemblance to a country wine, or to give the widest possible range of simple country wines imaginable. Both approaches are ill-conceived.

The grape is supreme and we cannot imitate it. And why should we? Our native fruits have their own characteristics which give us the opportunity to turn out splendid wines in their own right. A cellar stocked with a selection of the wines from this book should cater for every palate, but to achieve such a cellar the second approach of trying to make every conceivable wine to be found in a recipe book must be abandoned. You must be selective.

Making home-made wine is easy, but drinking the end-product is often not so easy. By searching for unusual recipes the beginner commonly finds himself labelling a succession of bottles of low quality wine, half-fermented wine and plainly revolting wine. It is only when it dawns on him that coffee wine, marigold wine and potato wine are not to his taste that he begins to be selective. He has reached the second stage of winemaking.

There are two fundamental approaches to winemaking nowadays and quite often there is a total barrier between them. The country winemaker scorns those who use kits and I suspect that the grape concentrate advocate is suspicious of "messy" country wines. It is principally this second barrier which I would like to see demolished. It seems a tragedy that many a box-bedroom houses 3 or 4

Delightful surprises await those who have not yet tried good country wines.

demijohns of imitation commercial "plonk" from grape concentrate without a single blackberry, elderberry or damson in sight. When a gallon jar is emptied it remains so until another tin of grape juice can be afforded. To those who have this attitude, I say: do try one of my suggested fruit recipes instead of leaving that jar empty. You will not be disappointed. I know people who drank keg beer for years simply because they had not bothered to try real ale!

For the majority who are already converted to the potential of the indigenous fruits of this country, my hope is that I can help you to avoid the mistakes I once made. There *is* a short-cut to experience. When I look back over old recipe jottings I realise how I wasted many an hour and 3lb. or so of sugar on a recipe which had no hope of success. Gradually one sheds individual recipes, methods of preparation and even whole classes of ingredients. My aim is to short-cut this painful process of reaching a selective attitude.

If it is controversial to dismiss many favourite wines as not worth making, then the chance has to be taken. The grounds for not only omitting normally accepted ingredients from the recommended recipes but even listing them as to be avoided are not purely subjective. There are good scientific grounds for saying that maize or pea pods do not make good wines. More importantly there is the common palate. There is absolutely no point in spending months trying to reproduce a concoction which grandmother used to make when your chances of something worthwhile are about one in twenty. Bear in mind that the "nectar" you recall might have been matured for six or eight years. Wines matured for that length of time are normally either awful or splendid, regardless of the starting ingredients.

Luck does come into winemaking. The difference between a good wine and a grand wine is very slight. That particularly good summer, that particularly well-balanced must, that perfect fermentation will happen every now and then. And that little bit of luck is necessary. However, if the difference between a good wine and a prizewinner is slight, the difference between a good wine and a poor wine is huge. If you can use recipes which give an excellent chance of a good wine, then that little bit of fortune will sometimes come along to grace you with an outstanding wine. Give your winemaking a chance.

8

CHAPTER 1

Myths and bad habits

There is a clutter of outdated ideas to be swept away before we can begin. A modern attitude to the hobby can give superb, consistent results, so let us brush away these cobwebs of the old. Persistent misconceptions still abound.

The raw, uncultured wines of the past should not have a place in our cellar. These days every town has its outlets for all the chemical and fruit additives which we need to make balanced wines. The days of carrot whisky made by floating a piece of toast spread with baker's yeast have long gone, but some of those images remain to prejudice people's thoughts.

Parsnip and beetroot wines were probably made in such great quantities in the past because of a surplus in the kitchen garden. It can be argued that they are not proper wines. The elderberry wine which your mother recalls as having been given to her as a cure for colds or 'flu was probably harsh or sickly — we can do much better with our elderberries.

If someone tells you that "potatoes make a strong wine" you realise what you are up against. You know very well that sugar gives the strength (i.e. alcohol) to wine and the potatoes, if they contribute anything, add only harshness and starch. But don't bother to explain. Give that person a glass of subtle fruit wine and see if he changes his ideas.

It has long been thought in some quarters that the objective of the home winemaker is to produce as lethal a dose of alcohol as possible, in whatever guise. Stories of knees buckling and heads swimming are still rife. The truth is that the "strength" of a country wine will normally be about the same as (perhaps slightly higher than) that of an import from France or Germany.

Complete kits for beginners can be purchased but equipment can be built up as required. Samples by courtesy of Kings Homebrew and Boots, Hemel Hempstead.

Using an excess of fruit is one of the ways in which you can contribute to the abuse of good winemaking. If someone gives you six pounds of damsons you have the alternative of making one bad gallon or two good gallons. There is absolutely no advantage in overloading a must with fruit just because it is available. The aim should be a well-balanced, even delicate, wine. The hobby is a craft which rewards care and attention.

Beware recipes which suggest $3\frac{1}{2}$ lbs of sugar or more. Beware recipes for dry wines from unsubtle ingredients – such as root vegetables or raspberries. In this book I have omitted a recipe for a dry wine where I consider it inappropriate for the main ingredient.

Two other common failings are oxidised wines and bottles which, when taken from the shelf, have a nasty deposit at the bottom or even a noticeable haze throughout the contents. Oxidisation gives a peculiar flavour and there is no excuse for it. If your wine is fermented under air lock and the water level in this air lock is checked occasionally the problem will be unlikely to arise. If you give your wine sufficient attention at the bottling stage, the incidence of deposits or haze should be rare.

Many advocates of wines from grape concentrates consider country wines to be messy and time-consuming. Certainly, if they hate the fresh air, hedgerows and the very thought of picking fruit, you might have difficulty in converting them. However, the basic pulp fermentation method described in this book is hardly messy and the time taken over a gallon of wine *from start to finish* can be estimated as follows:

Preparing the yeast starter and must	15 mins
Pitching the yeast etc.	2 mins
Straining off pulp into demijohn	10 mins
Racking (say 3 x 5)	15 mins
Fining/filtering and bottling	20 mins
Total	62 mins.

Each gallon of wine takes you about an hour of your leisure time, spread over a few months. The average cost of a bottle of wine from hedgerow or garden produce is around 15–20p.

The other argument is that the time from picking the fruit to drinking the wine is excessive. Grape concentrate kits are produced with a view to the fastest possible vin ordinaire in many cases and this seems, sadly, to have become the accepted requirement. You cannot make a quality wine quickly. You are creating something special and patience is part of the art.

Finally, it should be mentioned that you are likely to find an imbalance in the types of wine in your store cupboard or cellar if you use a full range of the recommended recipes. There will be a preponderance of reds. Do not worry about this – they cover such a range of types that there should be something to suit every taste. Our best indigenous fruits are mainly red.

CHAPTER 2

Equipment

It is unnecessary for you to surround yourself immediately with a large amount of expensive equipment. Over a number of years winemakers invariably accumulate all manner of different spoons, brushes and pieces of tubing, but a lot of the peripheral equipment you see can be acquired gradually, if at all.

The major investment necessary is in glass – demijohns, hydrometer and bottles – and the latter can be saved or scrounged from friends. It is normal to build up a stock of gallon jars, often up to 12 or 20, before considering oneself fully equipped.

We can usefully separate winemakers' equipment into three categories – essential, advisable and luxury.

ESSENTIAL

Scales You can, in fact, use any accurate kitchen scales for weighing ingredients.

Pulp Fermenting Vessel This sounds impressive, but is merely a 2 gallon white polythene or polypropylene bucket with a lid. A good one will last ten years. Buy from a specialist winemakers' supplier or multiple shop and make sure that the lid seals well. Do not be tempted to use a normal coloured domestic bucket – the colour dyes can contain harmful chemicals which will be leached out during fermentation. A basic piece of equipment like this wants choosing with care.

Pulper Obviously you require the juice from soft fruit and the skins will have to be burst before fermentation. Some use the flat bottom of a wine bottle to press down on the pulp, others a home-made piece of shaped hardwood. In fact, a potato masher is quite adequate for most jobs. Fruits which are less co-operative and need special attention are discussed in the individual recipes.

Sieve   An 8"–10" (20–25cm) sieve is required for straining the must into the gallon jar after the initial fermentation. It is sensible to have one set aside specifically for winemaking, rather than to use the one employed for sprouts.

Large Spoon   This should preferably be wooden or plastic. Your wine shop will have a range of sizes.

Gallon Demijohn   The familiar glass jar with "ears" can nowadays be seen everywhere. Although you only need a single demijohn initially, keep your eyes open for coloured demijohns because they are invaluable for red wines – otherwise you will need a cover or a cupboard for your clear jar if the wine is red.

Larger fermenters are available. Plastic 2 gallon containers with an air-lock fitted to the cap are excellent and have the advantage of being suitable for white or red wines. If you search around, you might also locate 5 gallon sizes. All of the recipes given in this book are for one gallon and you will obviously have to multiply the quantities of ingredients accordingly.

Air-lock and Bored Bung   These are also available in nearly every multiple shop. Be careful of glass air-locks – it is all too easy to sustain a nasty cut when forcing them into bungs.

Bungs can be either cork or rubber. Cork ones are cheaper, but they must be of best quality. Low grade cork can have so many holes in it that air can pass into the jar and this will give you problems of oxidisation. Rubber bungs are more expensive but are totally reliable. There was a school of thought that rubber bungs

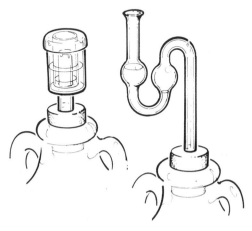

Glass air-locks and bored bungs

13

These fermentation bins are both in the larger, 5 ½ gallon category and are easily available from winemakers' shops and branches of multiple stores.

might taint the wine, but there is always a gap between the wine and the bung and I have never known this to happen in practice.

The equipment listed above will be sufficient to allow your wine to reach its fermentation jar.

For racking you will require:

Siphon Tubing   A 5 or 6 feet (up to 2m) length of standard tubing is required. Fancy ones can be purchased with a tap on one end and a tapering neck-piece to push into the top of your gallon jar. These are not necessary for normal racking, but they are considered by many to be superior for bottling. There are two things to remember. Firstly, the tubing should have a sufficient diameter to allow a steady flow of the wine (otherwise racking can become a tedious process). Secondly, it should be purpose-made, insofar that one end should be sealed and have two side holes (to prevent sediment being sucked into the tube too easily).

Spare Demijohn   For racking a second jar is required to receive the siphoned wine and hold it while the original is being cleaned.

For bottling a gallon you will need the following:

Everything you could possibly need is now available from winemakers'
suppliers but it is prudent to buy only as the need arises. The text gives
sound advice.

Bottle Brush   Look for a nylon brush which is long enough yet
slim enough to clean both bottles and demijohns.
Corks   Use only straight corks. Tapered or T-shaped are used
only for short-term or show purposes. This is one area where
economy can be false – the cheapest straight corks are sometimes
so inferior that they emit a murky deposit when knocked into the
bottle and your brilliantly clear wine becomes cloudy.
Corking Machine   The simplest form is not expensive. It is merely
a wooden or plastic sleeve and cap which compresses the cork to
enable it to be "flogged" home into the neck of the bottle. More
sophisticated "bench" types can also be purchased.
Wine Labels   of your choice.
Funnel   An 8"–10" (20–30cm) funnel, of white plastic or polypropylene, is invaluable for adding sugar syrup and moving small
amounts of wine between jars.
   I have deliberately left until last the most important tool of the
trade:
Hydrometer and Jar   To my mind it is ludicrous to get involved

in winemaking without a hydrometer. The simple, graduated float allows you to check on the gravity (and thus the residual sugar content) of your wine as it progresses. Without a hydrometer you will fail to distinguish between a wine which has fermented out and one which is continuing to ferment slowly. You will not be able to recognise a stuck fermentation. It will enable you to avoid bottling wines which might explode in the cellar.

A wine hydrometer is marked from around 0.980 up to 1.160 and the key figure is 1.000, which is the specific gravity of water at 20°C. When you have prepared your must (all the pulp, sugar and starting ingredients) you can take an initial reading. Pour a quantity of the must into the jar and float the hydrometer in it. Take a reading of the mark where the surface of the liquid "cuts" the scale, by looking along the surface of the must. This will be the Original Gravity of your wine.

As the fermentation proceeds you can take a hydrometer reading every time you rack and make a note of it. A look back to your note of the Specific Gravity when you last racked will give you a clear picture of progress within the demijohn. Towards the end it will also tell you whether the wine is likely to have finished fermenting and be ready for bottling. A constant reading over 4–6 weeks at the expected finishing point will suggest that this is the case.

A dry wine should finish below 1.000. Obviously if you find that your intended sweet wine has dropped to such a level you will want to add more sugar syrup to increase the S.G. and restart the fermentation. In broad terms your aim for finishing readings should be:

Sweet, dessert wines	1.015–1.020
Normal medium to sweet	1.010–1.015
Medium sweet	around 1.005
Medium dry	around 1.000
Dry	below 1.000

Do not use this as a definite guide – tastes vary, particularly with regard to the amount of residual sugar in sweet and dessert wines. For dry wines a finishing gravity as low as 0.980 is often sought for show purposes.

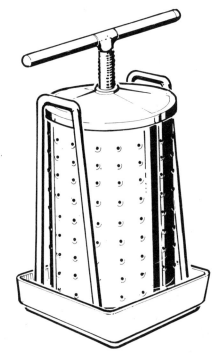

*Left, hydrom-
eter and jar.*

*Right, one
form of wine
press.*

ADVISABLE EQUIPMENT

Notebook If you keep a recipe book and record your wines as
you make them, you will be able to consider the ingredients when
you are drinking that wine. It can be repeated or improved upon
at a future date. This aspect is dealt with in more detail later.

Thermometer A winemaker's or brewer's thermometer will enable
you to check the temperature of your new must so that you are
certain of introducing the yeast at the right time.

Finings Wine finings will often work wonders on hazes and can
be purchased as and when necessary. The treatment will, however,
leave a loose sediment and bottling can be difficult without disturbing this, unless you rack carefully. I much prefer a filter system,
but it is sometimes necessary to fine before filtering if the finished
wine is particularly cloudy.

Filter It is tempting to put a filter in the class of essential equipment. Why invest time and money in a wine if at the end of

17

the day you bottle a cloudy end-product? This has been a sad characteristic of home-made wine over the years – a layer of silt eventually to be seen over the bottom of the bottle. When you can afford it, purchase a filter system. The basic idea is that you rack your wine from one gallon jar to another through a vessel which filters the wine. The filter pad is renewable. One word of warning – check the price and availablity of the appropriate pads before purchasing. The long-term cost is in the "software".

LUXURY EQUIPMENT

There is a great deal of pricey paraphernalia available to you and some of it is of limited value.

Fruit Juice Extractor   These are not cheap but are particularly useful in extracting liquids from difficult fruits, such as apples.

Wine Press   Various types are advertised. All of them work on the principle of exerting pressure on the pulp by means of a screw. They enable you to extract the maximum from your pulp at the sieving stage.

Plastic Mincer   Most households have a mincer made of metal, but for contact with soft fruits a plastic one is better. For example, sultanas can be prepared for the must without any danger of them picking up a metallic tang.

Scientific Test Kits   Acid testing kits (and the cheaper alternatives) are dealt with later.

Generally, do not be misled into thinking that every new piece of equipment or fancy dispensing gadget is a boon to the winemaker. Practise caution.

CHAPTER 3

Cleaning and Sterilising

Cleanliness is absolutely essential in winemaking and the habit of cleaning equipment both before and after use should be acquired. Bear in mind that you are dealing with raw fruit in the initial stages and there can hardly be anything more prone to infection from all manner of air-borne bacteria and insects. You only increase that risk by using dirty equipment.

Your aim should be either to sulphite early or to achieve a very quick initial fermentation, so that your must is protected by a layer of carbon dioxide. That should take care of external threats to your wine and your problems of hygiene will then be confined to the equipment itself.

After you have strained your pulp into the gallon jar (the actual method is dealt with later) your fermentation bucket must be sterilised thoroughly. Similarly funnels, brushes and demijohns need attention before and after use. The tubing employed in racking (siphoning) is often forgotten in this list of items which need frequent cleaning. A quick rinse through with tap water is not sufficient.

Boiling water has very limited uses. It can be rinsed, with care, around your fermentation bucket and funnel. But glass and plastics will break or distort, and you do not want shattered demijohns or a spiral of bent tubing.

You will have to turn to chemical cleansing agents. There are so many different brands available that it is necessary to look at the types individually:

Sodium Metabisulphite (including Campden Tablets)
One of the cheapest methods is to use diluted sodium metabisulphite (in crystal form or as Campden tablets) together with a

little citric acid. These agents are commonly recommended, but they should be used with **extreme caution**.

The sterilising function is by the gas given off by these chemicals and the fumes which achieve this are very pungent. A whiff of sulphur dioxide is not pleasant and the solution should be prepared at arm's length and kept in closed containers. If you suffer from any respiratory problems **do not use** this method. Asthma attacks have been known to be brought on by inhaling these fumes, so be careful. If you are in any doubt, try an alternative method.

Chempro SDP

This is a readily available sterilising agent, sold by the multiple stores, and full instructions are set out on the packet. The dangers of inhalation are not present here. It can be used with confidence. Chempro not only sterilises but also assists in removing deposits.

Other Brewery Descalers

Some specialist wine and beer shops sell a liquid descaler which

Some of the more easily obtained chemical sterilisers which are recommended. Many winemakers deliberately leave a trace to improve the wine.

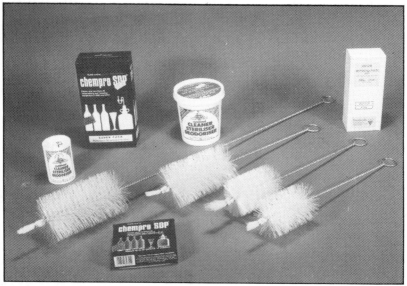

is used for cleaning fermentation vessels in breweries. Ritchie Products' "Winemaster PPH" is an example. These liquid descalers are excellent, for they have the ability to remove yeast films and moulds at the same time as sterilising. The viscous liquid is diluted and can be used several times. It operates by contact rather than fumes. It has a distinctive oily feel to the touch and care should be taken in handling glass items which have been soaked in the solution, as they may be slippery.

V.W.P. Cleaner/Steriliser

This is another excellent and safe product which is readily available.

Milton

Gentle but effective sterilisation is obviously the criterion of a product used in the nursery. It can be useful to us and I know that many winemakers rely upon it. The only reservation to be made is that Milton (and other similar products) has an appreciable and distinctive smell which will not worry an infant but which might taint a wine. Rinse your sterilised equipment very thoroughly before using it again.

Others

The above list is not exhaustive and just because a product is omitted does not mean that it is inferior. Several other commercially produced sterilising agents will do the job. However, read the packaging for instructions and any warnings before you buy.

CHAPTER 4

Yeasts and Chemical Additives

YEASTS

There is a bewildering range of yeasts available. Many varieties of wine types can be purchased in liquid, tablet or powder form. Some require starting with sugar and acid, others are simply sprinkled onto the must and stirred in. Use a general purpose yeast as your basic fermenter. If you are intent upon using a named wine yeast, advice is given in the recipes.

C.W.E. Formula 67 yeast compound is in my experience an extremely reliable standby. It can be purchased in individual sachets or in a small tub. The yeast is already mixed with sufficient sugar and nutrients for a vigorous fermentation to be commenced simply by mixing it with water. Place a teaspoon of C.W.E. yeast compound into cool (ideally 65°F) water in a sterilised bottle and plug the neck. Leave it an hour or two and you will see signs of activity sufficient for you to add it to your must with confidence. *Proferma* general purpose yeast will give similar results.

The thing to avoid at all costs is a yeast which will be sluggish in beginning to multiply and ferment the wine. It is worth repeating that your must is at its most vulnerable until it is fermenting strongly. If you do purchase a fancy yeast type (particularly those sold in liquid form in miniature test tubes) make certain that you have a very active fermentation in your yeast starter before you prepare the fruit etc. for your must.

At all costs avoid anything which might not be a true wine yeast. Also, be careful of powder or tablet yeasts which are recommended to be sprinkled or crumbled into the must. You want as robust a yeast as you can get, searching for the sugar in your fermentation bucket from the moment you pitch it in to do its work. It really needs pre-starting to be able to do this.

NUTRIENT SALTS

The addition of nutrients will give you a more reliable fermentation. They are readily available and the appropriate "dose" is usually made clear in the instructions. They are principally ammonium salts. The diluted fruit juice which forms the basis of your must will contain its own nutrients, but they will often be sufficient only to take the fermentation to a certain point. To avoid a wine which is oversweet and low in alcohol the addition of nutrients in the must is an easy and cheap standard practice.

On the same shelf as these nutrient salts you will often see yeast energisers. The recipes in this book should not give rise to the need for an energiser, unless you want to try one with a stuck fermentation (a subject which is dealt with separately later). There is no need, in the normal course of events, to bother with an energiser. It is only really necessary for "thin" musts, a characteristic avoided by these recipes.

An assortment of available yeasts, nutrients and allied materials.

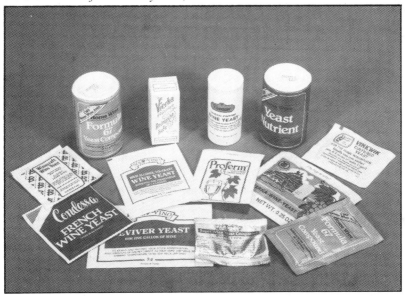

On the other hand, vitamin B tablets are a useful additive. Yeasts need this vitamin to thrive, so if you can find a packet of these tiny tablets, buy them (they are not expensive and a packet will last many months). In the past it was common to add a teaspoon of Marmite to the must. A single vitamin B tablet to each gallon merely provides the modern alternative. To find them you will probably have to search out a specialist home brew shop. If you fail to locate them, bear in mind that they are desirable rather than essential.

PECTIN-DESTROYING ENZYMES

Certain fruits contain an excess of pectin, which is very useful for setting jam but a nuisance if you want a clear wine. If you use peaches or plums, for instance, without adding an enzyme to break down the high level of pectin, you will end up with a cloudy wine which will not fine or filter. There are plenty of liquids or powders available to do the job and full instructions are usually given with them. Add one or two teaspoons of *Pectolase*, or the like, when you are about to pitch the yeast. Do not expose enzymes to high temperatures. You can use pectolase in every must if you wish, but the recipes in this book give an indication of which fruits need it.

GRAPE TANNIN

A well balanced wine needs a quantity of tannin to give it that little "bite". An extract of tea used to be the answer. Now we can purchase tannin in liquid or powder form and the latter is probably the most economical. Most white wines which we make are particularly deficient in this respect and it is advisable to have tannin available. The objective is not a perfect imitation of the grape, merely an acceptable balance in the wine.

CAMPDEN TABLETS

These tablets of sodium metabisulphite have become widely used in home winemaking – too much so, in my opinion. They are of course merely a measured and convenient dose of the same chemical that is used for sterilising equipment. Common times of use are as follows:

Sulphiting the Must	— this is a precautionary way of preparing fruit before fermentation.
Temporary Storage	— fruit can be kept free from infection if you keep it in a solution of one Campden tablet to every 3lbs of the fruit for a few days until you can use it.
Racking	— some winemakers always sulphite their wine after racking. To my mind this is not necessary and can retard the yeast.
Stopping	— Campden tablets are used in conjunction with a wine stabiliser at bottling time to be sure that no further fermentation will occur in the bottle.

Although the amount of sodium metabisulphite being used is much less than for sterilising, it is as well to treat the fumes with care, particularly if you have respiratory problems.

Campden tablets are dissolved in warm water before adding to the fruit or wine. If you stir the solution into a bucket of fruit there will be a bleaching effect — do not worry about this, as it is temporary only.

CHAPTER 5

Adjuncts to your basic fruit

As winemaking has become more sophisticated it has also become unduly complicated. One of the areas of unnecessary complication is that of adjuncts to fruit recipes — grape concentrate, raisins or sultanas, lemons, bananas, honey and dried flowers are all listed in long-winded recipes. They need to be examined one by one to investigate their worth.

The reason for the use of adjuncts is two-fold. Some wines lack substance in themselves. Three pounds or so of many fruits produce only a diluted juice which has insufficient body. There is an obvious need to incorporate some other ingredient which will rectify this. Do not be tempted to increase the fruit because your first attempt lacks body — the likely result will be an overpowering flavour and probably an excessive level of acidity.

The other reason for using an adjunct arises where your prime ingredient would not in itself ferment properly. An obvious example is ginger wine.

GRAPE CONCENTRATE
Commercial fruit wines invariably include grape. It enables the manufacturer to produce a consistent product from year to year. In the past two decades it has become accepted practice for the home enthusiast to follow suit and you will see many books in which every recipe contains grape.

But is our aim the same as that of the mass-producer? The cost of consistency is to deny the excellent. If you create the average (albeit an acceptably good average) by using such concentrates all the time, you are denying yourself the chance of superb wines from our own fruits. You can tell whether a wine is based upon grape concentrate at first taste and there is a danger that we are moving towards grape wines which just happen to have a country flavouring.

One of the objectives of this little book is to demonstrate that some of our better fruits (and mixes of them) stand proudly as excellent wine-making ingredients in their own right. We do not have to imitate the grape.

Having got that off my chest, there are some wines and types of wines which benefit from a measure of grape concentrate and I am not advocating a total abandonment of the practice. Used carefully it can be incorporated into some wines to great effect, principally as a more refined (but more expensive) alternative to sultanas and banana as a means of adding body to a thin must. However, do not be tempted to buy a "vin ordinaire" type of concentrate. If you are using grape juice, buy only the best. To complete the must for a quality country wine by adding cheap grape concentrate is nothing less than criminal.

About half a can which is designed for a gallon of grape wine (or 1 pint – 550ml) will be sufficient as an additive. The remainder can be stored in a polythene bag in the freezer (but be careful to seal the bag carefully because grape concentrate can be reluctant to freeze and sometimes only goes "mushy").

The argument is that grape concentrate gives you a steady fermentation and adds "vinosity" to a wine. Treat this assertion with some caution. However, if you insist upon using it as a regular additive you can substitute grape concentrate for sultanas in any of the recipes where they appear. The adjustments required if you do so are explained in more detail later. Basically 1 pint (550ml) of grape juice will reduce your fruit requirements by $\frac{1}{2}$ lb (225g) and the sugar similarly.

Over recent years mini-cans of grape concentrate have appeared on the shelves of multiple shops. These are designed specifically for adding to country recipes. However, my experiments with these small cans have proved rather disappointing. They are cheap and you might want to try them. No adjustments are required to the recipe if you add the contents of a mini-can, as their effect will not be pronounced on sugar or acidity.

The use of grape concentrate is sometimes put forward as an easy way to assured success. It is useful at times, but I still maintain that it can bring a "sameness" to our wines at the expense of the real art of the hobby. Do not forget that a wine made solely from grape concentrate would have about the same effect on a European vintner as dehydrated potato would have on a gourmet.

SULTANAS AND RAISINS

Many more traditional recipes include large quantities of different varieties of dried grape. The reason is obvious – they provide a cheap and fairly easy way of extracting grape juice. However, the flavour is not always reliable and they should be treated with a little care. As an adjunct they are fine, as a basis for a wine they are often poor.

Currants are inferior and should be avoided. Use only sultanas or raisins. Because I prefer sultanas I have named them in the recipes, but you can substitute good quality raisins if you wish. In fact, raisins are often recommended for red wines. Do not buy small fruit, such as that found in boxes for cake-making. Select large sultanas or raisins from health food shops or winemakers' suppliers and check for any sign of mould (they are usually in cellophane wrappers nowadays).

Dried fruits such as sultanas have a definite place in winemaking.

I always use a reasonable amount of sultanas in ginger wine. Obviously crushed root ginger will not in itself support a fermentation and the sultanas give that facility without unduly affecting the end-product. Ginger has an overpowering flavour in itself, of course, and sultanas are cheaper than grape concentrate.

The problem is that if you are making a delicate wine sultanas or raisins can impair the flavour. It can become predominantly a sultana or raisin wine. Nevertheless, they are very useful for a little body and for giving a boost to your fermentation.

Use them in quantities of $\frac{1}{2}$ lb (225g) as a standard measure and prepare them carefully. Wash the fruit and then mince or chop, so that the goodness within can be leached out during the pulp fermentation. If you have only an old metal domestic mincer, be cautious. A plastic one is better. In fact, if you do not have a plastic mincer, it is probably best to settle for chopping by hand. The larger varieties make this task much easier. You do not have to slice them into minute pieces – a rough cut through the middle will do.

BANANAS

I have no hesitation in recommending bananas. They give body to the wine without disturbing the flavour unduly. In addition, they are easy to prepare and relatively cheap. Many of our more acidic fruits or those with a strong flavour, when diluted to acceptable proportions, produce a rather insubstantial wine. The addition of bananas (or "banana gravy" as it is sometimes called) can remedy this fault.

Buy either ripe, fresh bananas or dried bananas (as sold by health food shops). Do not use the chipped dried fruit of the type that is found in tropical fruit mixes. Your fresh bananas should be beginning to blacken on the skins (in fact, your greengrocer might well sell you over-ripe bananas at a discount!) Do not use "green" bananas. The dried variety tends to be consistent, but you must be careful to judge the amount required. The shrinkage involved in drying bananas is such that it is easy to overdo the dose. Remember that each little dried banana represents a whole fresh one – three or four are a maximum to the gallon.

Preparation is by boiling. The liquor from the banana and not the actual pulp itself is poured into the must. Slice your bananas

Bananas supply the body which may be lacking in some musts; lemons and oranges are best kept for specific wine, as on page 66.

into water in about $\frac{1}{2}$"–1" (2cm) lengths and simmer them for ten minutes or so. The boil should not be for so long that it allows the fruit to break up into the water. This collapse into "mush" can occur with ripe, fresh fruit at about 10–15 minutes. With dried fruit you can boil safely for 15 minutes.

LEMONS AND ORANGES

To adjust for acid, the addition of the juice of one or two lemons or oranges was often recommended in old recipes. You can forget this practice. A teaspoon of acid crystals is the modern alternative. In fact, a range of acids is readily available to the winemaker. The subtle differences between these acids leads us towards scientific winemaking, which this book attempts to keep to a minimum, but an equal mix of citric and tartaric acids or citric acid on its own will be perfectly satisfactory for normal use. Malic acid, which is the familiar acid of apples, can also be purchased, but it is of lesser value to us.

FLOWERS

The incorporation of fresh or dried flowers (for bouquet, of course) into musts has been popular for at least twenty years. To my mind it is an over-rated practice. Certainly, if you are blending several ingredients in your recipe or trying to make your wine that little bit different for an exhibition class, two handfuls of rose petals or a large pinch of dried elderflower might be a worthwhile experiment, but if you are making one of the sound, individualistic wines recommended by this book, forget about trying to interfere with the natural bouquet.

"Nose" is very important, of course, but a fruit of any worth has its own characteristics in this respect. So much so, in fact, that I have gradually convinced myself that you can tell a potentially good wine at a very early stage by using your sense of smell. When you sieve your wine off the pulp (lees) into the gallon jar you can detect promise. Over and above the carbon dioxide in the air there can be a sweet, "winey" odour which fills you with justifiable optimism – this is surely the natural bouquet of the wine and it is not based upon dried flowers.

HONEY

If you like mead, ferment about 3 lbs (1350g) of carefully selected honey and rely upon your patience. If you want a fruit wine, then do not bother to interfere with it by adding honey.

This is not the "official line", I know, but really honey can only disturb the characteristics of flavour that we are striving for in these recipes. If you have hives or a cheap supply, restrict your use of honey to white wines, substituting it for a proportion of the sugar. If you are not so fortunate, experiment with honey in recipes if you must, but do not use it as a regular adjunct.

CHAPTER 6

Picking and freezing

"Gather your fruit on a sunny day" is familiar advice, and justifiably so. The quality of your raw materials is important and rain- or even dew-affected berries are normally inferior. To combine a pleasant evening or Sunday afternoon with a little picking is the way to enjoy winemaking.

Another adage warns against picking (blackberries, in particular) in October. The fruit is said to have been tainted by the devil! Whereas there is no scientific evidence of this effect, like most "old wives' tales" it hides a grain of truth. The cold nights of late autumn cause deterioration and the softer fruits should not be picked after September. There are a few exceptions – sloes and rosehips, for instance, might not ripen properly in some parts of the country until October or even November.

Pick only ripe fruit. Elderberries should be hanging down, full as if ready to burst. Blackberries should be very black. If your fingers are not stained after gathering red fruit, you have failed to find well-ripened berries. Better to use a lesser amount of quality material than a randomly picked larger quantity. The ultimate potential of your wine will be governed by the quality of its basic ingredient.

Do not pick close to a main road. The lead content of petrol is such that heavy traffic may have affected the fruit. Accumulations of lead are obviously to be avoided and those inviting banks of brambles alongside major roads could harbour dangers. Exhaust fumes impair flavour in any case. Also avoid picking near quarries or similar situations where a large amount of dust is thrown up, as this may be difficult to remove by rinsing. Obviously the best sites are off the beaten track or close to quiet country lanes.

If you have picked away from home (when visiting or on holiday, for instance), you need a means of keeping your fruit in good condition until you can use it. The answer is to sulphite. Use one Campden tablet per 3lbs (1350g) of fruit and dissolve this in warm water (bearing in mind the caution regarding inhalation of the fumes). Dilute the sulphite in sufficient water to cover the fruit and keep in a closed container – a demijohn with a solid bung will suffice. You will then be able to use the sterilised fruit as and when you want.

When you bring fresh spoils home, wash them thoroughly in running cold water. There may be a few tiny insects or grubs which are not welcome. For an instant wine, the berries can go directly into the fermentation bucket for sulphiting or for the hot syrup treatment, both of which methods are described in the following chapter. If you are freezing for future use, dry the berries as well as you can by rolling them in a tea cloth.

For those who have a freezer autumn should be an industrious time. Gather as many of our indigenous fruits as you can so that you can make wines throughout the winter from quality hedgerow pickings. Garden produce and fruits which have been purchased at their cheapest and best in the shops (e.g. cherries or pulp removed from peaches) can also be frozen.

Do not bag your fruit indiscriminately for freezing. Use pre-weighed quantities of 1 lb, 1½ lb or 2 lb (450g, 675g or 900g), so that you can extract the required amount for a gallon at any time without having to chip away at a large block of frozen fruit or pulp.

Mark the bags which are going into the freezer with the name of the contents (it can be difficult to tell a loganberry from a blackberry and certainly a cultivated blackberry from a wild one) and with the pre-frozen weight. Add a comment on your label as to quality – "class 1" elderberries should be reserved for pure elderberry wines whereas slightly inferior fruit can be used in mixes with, for instance, blackberries.

CHAPTER 7

The basic method

Everyone develops his or her own way of preparing a must and conducting the fermentation. However, there are so many different methods – sulphiting, long pulp fermentations, short pulp fermentations, liquidising, juice extraction by special enzymes etc. – that it is tempting to move from one system to another without ever establishing a consistent approach.

A lot of the elaborate methods are unnecessary. The basic choice is between sulphiting and immersion in hot liquid. Incidentally, do not be tempted to boil your fruit as a means of sterilising it – you will end up with stewed apple or stewed blackberry wine. If you prepare your must carefully and introduce a very vigorous yeast at the right time there is little chance of a disaster. Within a matter of hours your fermentation should be under way and a protective blanket of carbon dioxide will be present as your safeguard.

The gradual addition of sugar, starting with 1 lb (450g) and adding the balance in $\frac{1}{2}$ lb (225g) lots as and when the gravity reaches dryness (i.e. SG around 1.000) is certainly an advantage in one way. The system encourages maximum alcohol and gives the yeast a steady feed. If you are the type of winemaker who is able to make a check on the progress of your wines every week or two, then use this "instalment" plan. However, the loss incurred in taking the short-cut of adding all of the sugar at the start of fermentation is not great. A further $\frac{1}{2}$ lb (225g) can always be added eventually to a proposed sweet wine if your hydrometer tells you so.

To start a dry wine with $2\frac{1}{2}$ lb (1125g) of sugar will give you the likelihood of a crisp, dry wine – the instalment plan is not really necessary. The argument sometimes put forward is that you run a greater risk of a stuck fermentation if you include all of the sugar initially. In truth, providing that you have a well-balanced must, this risk is slight. Stuck fermentations and their cures are dealt with in detail later.

Always bear in mind that certain ingredients contain a high proportion of sugar in themselves (sultanas, raisins and grape concentrate are obvious examples) and in designing recipes their sugar content equivalent must be deducted from the 2½–3 lb (1125–1350g) approach. In fact, almost all fruits have a certain amount of sugar of their own, but the standard quantities of sugar addition are compatible with most fruits in normal use.

On balance, the busy winemaker can adopt the straightforward method of including all of the sugar in the recipe at the onset. It makes life far simpler.

1) PREPARATION OF THE MUST

(a) Fresh Fruit

Wash the fruit carefully and discard any inferior berries. Sprinkle a layer evenly over the bottom of the bucket and mash with a suitable implement. Add another layer, mash again and continue so doing until it has all been broken down. Place the bucket on one side, making sure that it is well covered.

Put the sugar in a saucepan and just cover with cold water. Bring this to the boil, stirring occasionally, and remove from the heat as soon as you have clear syrup. Do not prolong the boil, or you will end up with toffee. Pour the hot sugar syrup over the crushed fruit.

If you are using bananas, boil them in a pint or so of water for the recommended length of time (see Chapter 4). Strain off the liquor, discard the fruit and add the liquor to the must. Cover the fermentation bucket again. Make your yeast starter at this point. If a yeast compound (such as C.W.E. Formula 67) is being used, all you need to do is to place one or two teaspoons in a clean glass or bottle and add water at about 65°F (the temperature is not critical to a few degrees, but bear in mind that if it is near to blood heat the yeast may be killed). In practice, if you take a normal half-pint glass, half-fill with cold water from the tap and merely take the chill off this with a small amount of hot water from the kettle, the yeast will be happy. Cover the glass and place in a warm position. If you are using a pure yeast, you will have to make your own starter medium and any of the following are suitable:

1) A teaspoon of sugar and a pinch of citric acid, dissolved.
2) The juice of one lemon and a dissolved teaspoon of sugar.
3) A teaspoon of yeast extract, dissolved in the water.

Place the yeast starter on one side to begin its work. When your must is at the right temperature and the yeast starter is showing signs of activity (this can be two hours or so with a pure yeast, a minimum of an hour with a compound) you are ready to start the fermentation. Pour the yeast starter into the must and add all other ingredients (chemicals, acids and nutrients). Mix well. Cover your fermentation bucket well and put it in a warm place for the pulp fermentation.

The total volume of content of your bucket should be a gallon at this stage. A little less is quite acceptable. But if you add water to a level of much more than a gallon you might have too much at sieving stage. Even though you are going to decrease the starting volume at that time (by removing the pulp) you will need a little leeway to allow you to rinse the pulp before you discard it.

(b) Frozen Fruit

You have a choice of pre-thawing your frozen fruit (by moving it to the refrigerator 12–24 hours before you need it) or of going directly to the bucket in a frozen state. In some ways frozen fruit is better than fresh for winemaking. The process of freezing breaks down the tissues to some extent and makes extraction of juice easier. Frozen gooseberries, for instance, mash far more readily than fresh ones.

If you have thawed your fruit first, the method will be the same as for fresh, above. If you are going directly from the freezer to the fermentation bucket, you are likely to have lumps of frozen fruit. Place them in the bucket and pour the hot liquor(s) over them. Cover and leave to attain room temperature while the yeast starter is developing.

Your must will probably level out at a very low temperature initially and will need a warm position while the rapid thaw is continued. When it reaches about 65–70°F mash the fruit. Layering will not be necessary, as most fruits from the freezer break up easily.

Add the yeast and other ingredients, stir and cover well.

(c) Special Fruits

Certain ingredients, such as rhubarb, oranges and grapefruit, require a special method. The above mashing techniques will only work for soft, fleshy fruits. Similarly fruits of the "drupe" type (damsons, plums, greengages etc.) give special problems because of their stones – you can be left with a nutty flavour.

In these cases the basic method is adapted to their needs in the individual recipes.

The Case for Sulphiting

Sterilisation of fruit by the use of sodium metabisulphite (usually in the form of Campden tablets) is widely used by winemakers. It ensures that the fruit will not be attacked during the aerobic days of the wine's life. The method of pulp fermentation above, on the other hand, relies upon sterilisation by very hot syrups and I have had no failure with it in many years. Nevertheless such a system will have its critics.

If you are in the habit of sulphiting, then continue to do so. If you are the ultra-cautious newcomer, then by all means adopt the precaution of using one Campden tablet (dissolved in warm water) per 3 lbs (1350g) of fruit. You dilute the solution in enough water to cover the fruit and leave it for a few hours before making up your must.

The essence of the argument for sulphiting is that it guarantees sterilisation, whereas my immersion method is considered by some to be hit or miss. However, if you wash your berries thoroughly and reject any signs of mould or damage, crush them well and totally immerse in near-boiling syrups, you should not have problems. This is always providing, of course, that you have a virulent yeast. The performance of the yeast is the essence. In my opinion the presence of sulphite can inhibit the yeast initially – keep the "dose" to a minimum.

Sulphiting or immersion in hot liquid? – the choice is yours.

2) PULP FERMENTATION

Think in terms of five to seven days as the ideal length of your initial fermentation. If you are using drupes (fruits with large stones) or highly acid ingredients you may need to reduce it to three to five days.

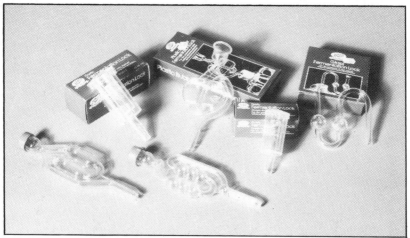

Fermentation air-locks in both glass and plastic. The two basic types are the concentric cylinder (top left) and twin-bulb U shape (top right). All are widely available from winemakers' suppliers or multiple stores.

The wine does need regular attention during these early days. Stir your pulp at least once a day. The carbon dioxide will have pushed a crust of fruit to the surface, which will dry out and become vulnerable and rather unpleasant if you do not mix it back into the body of the liquid regularly.

After your 5–7 days it is time to strain the wine off the solids. You will need a jug, spoon, strainer and, of course a gallon demijohn with bung and air-lock. Strain by the jugful through the sieve, which rests in the funnel, into the gallon jar. Press each batch of pulp lightly with the back of a spoon and rinse with a small amount of water. Do not over-rinse, as your aim is not to fill the demijohn. If you end up with a jar which is only three-quarters full you can add cold water, but leave at least a 2–2½ inch (5–6cm) air gap above the surface of the wine. Discard the fruit pulp.

An air-lock and bung can then be fitted into the neck of your demijohn. Do not fill your air-lock (especially the cylindrical upright type). The amount of water necessary is merely about $\frac{1}{2}$–$\frac{3}{4}$ inch (2cm) – sufficient to make a seal between the two "sleeves" of the lock without overflowing every time a gas bubble passes through. With a U-shaped lock, merely add enough water to half-fill the two "bulbs".

Bear in mind at this point that red wines will become brown wines if they are exposed to light for prolonged periods. If you are making a red wine you require either a coloured (usually brown) glass demijohn or some sort of covering. An easy way to do this is to use a plastic shopping carrier (any colour, rather than clear, will do) – you simply cut a hole in the middle of the bottom of the bag, turn it over and pull it around the demijohn like an overcoat. The air-lock and ears of the jar will protrude from the hole which you have cut. If you are using a polythene fermentation jar (such as the two gallon type with an air-lock fitted to the screw cap), you will not need any extra protection for red wines.

Place your new wine in a warm place (by a radiator in winter is ideal), but be cautious of it in the early stages. There will be a fair amount of pulp residue in your jar and the fermentation may be vigorous for a time. Either keep your eye on the demijohn for a few days or place it on a tray for about a week. Occasionally the fermentation will be so strong that pulp residue and wine will be pushed up through the air-lock. This is not a normal occurrence, but it can happen if you have left insufficient air gap in the jar. Should the problem arise, it will be short-lived but dramatic. Wash and sterilise the air-lock and bung. Refit as soon as the excitement has subsided.

3) THE MAIN FERMENTATION AND RACKING

Your wine will need racking after two or three weeks and then at approximately monthly intervals as the main fermentation proceeds. Apart from the first racking, the timing of your attention is not critical.

The principal of racking is simply gravity siphoning. You will require an empty gallon jar (if you do not have one use your fermentation bucket) and a siphon tube. Position the full demijohn at a level at least 2 feet (60cm) above the clean, empty jar. Push the correct end of the siphon tube (usually stopped and having two side holes) into the top jar and ease it down into the young wine. For the first racking, the object is to avoid transferring much of the pulp (lees) into the other gallon jar. Have a look at the wine and judge where to stop the siphon tube in its downward push so that only a little pulp will be moved. The holes in the side of the siphon should be a fraction above the layer of heavy sediment. For racking at later stages you can push the siphon tube almost to the bottom of the demijohn and even tilt the jar slightly for maximum extraction.

Suck on the bottom of the tube to begin the flow of wine and push the lower end into the empty jar. Allow the wine to flow from one to the other, holding the tube in position.

Wash the debris from the top jar and clean it well, using a bottle brush if necessary. Before returning the wine to its original jar take a reading with your hydrometer. If you simply drop the hydrometer into the gallon jar it will either crash to the bottom and break or, at best, it will be difficult to retrieve. You need a purpose-made hydrometer jar or, failing that, a clean milk bottle which has been set aside and sterilised. Make a note of the specific gravity of your wine. Reading the hydrometer and recording the data will be found in the appropriate chapters.

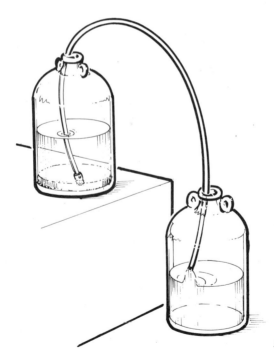

Racking

Transfer the wine back to its original container either by siphoning again or simply by pouring via a funnel (a little oxidisation will not hurt). Obviously you will have reduced the contents of the jar. Unless you need to make a sugar addition, you can top up with cold water to within an inch or two of the bottom of the neck of the demijohn. If the wine is an intended sweet one and the specific gravity has fallen to around 1.000 you will need to top up by adding the syrup of 4 oz. (115g) of sugar when it is cool.

Monthly racking will give you a very good idea of the progress of your wines. Additional sugar can be fed to sweet wines and an intended dry wine can be allowed to ferment as far below 1.000 as possible. In addition your racking will encourage wines to clear.

Wine will finish fermentation (and thus the hydrometer readings will stop reducing) in one of three ways:

1) It has fermented to dryness, there being no more fermentable sugar to feed the yeast (dry wine);
2) the yeast has reached a point where it can go no further due to the level of alcohol, leaving a stable wine with residual sugar (sweet wine);
3) the yeast is inhibited in some way, leaving a partially fermented, over-sweet wine (stuck fermentation).

Obviously the position of 1) or 2) is to be desired, that of 3) is a problem. Most of the recipes in this book will minimise the chances of a stuck fermentation, but they do occur. One secret is always to use a good yeast. It is the hydrometer which leads you to recognise the problem. If an intended dry wine drops below 1.000 or an intended sweet wine stops around 1.015–1.110 then it is merely a question of making certain that it is stable. Check that wine a month later with the hydrometer in order to be sure. If you find repeated hydrometer readings in the range of 1.030–1.020 you might well have a stuck fermentation. The subject, including cures, is dealt with in a separate chapter.

Bear in mind that all of the above is based upon the demijohn being in a fairly warm place (above 50°F). If it is February and you have your wine in a cold bedroom you might be experiencing merely a pause in the fermentation process – wait until March or April and see if things start to happen again.

4) CLEARING AND BOTTLING

We have stability – now we require clarity. There should not be too many problems from these well-balanced recipes, but if you do have a cloudy or stubbornly hazy wine, try wine finings. These are readily available and easy to use. Liquid finings are the best and the package will give a recommended dose per gallon. Simply mix this amount into about half a cup of the wine and pour it into the demijohn. Give the jar a swirl and leave for a few days. When the finings have settled, rack the good wine off the sediment.

You have either naturally clear wine or fined wine and you can bottle at this stage if you wish. However, it seems criminal, after all the care you have lavished on the wine, if you bottle it without ensuring a sparkling clarity. For this final polish you will need a filter system. There are plenty of different types on the market, but do heed my warning about the cost of replacement pads.

One gallon of wine makes 6 20cl bottles of wine, but if you have fined you may be down to $5\frac{1}{2}$ bottles or so. Your $\frac{1}{2}$ bottle can go directly into the decanter as "blackberry nouveau" or the like, or you can find a litre size as your fifth bottle. Straight corks should be used. Do not purchase cheap corks because they can emit a murky deposit when fitted.

Soak the corks for an hour or two in cold (not hot) water, sterilise bottles and then remove excess moisture from the wet corks with a clean tea towel. They are knocked into the neck of the bottles by tapping them through a simple corker with a light hammer. Tap them home firmly so that none of the cork protrudes.

We will consider storage, labelling and the like at a later stage.

CHAPTER 8

Recording and Monitoring your Wines

A simple system of numbering and recording your wines will pay considerable dividends. At the low price of just an odd few moments of your time you can move from a casual to a controlled approach.

Firstly, number your wines. If you give the year a letter and each wine a number to attach to that letter, then all you need is a small label on your demijohn during fermentation, showing that code, and eventually a little note similarly on each label when you bottle. Your "Elderberry A2" can be traced back at any time to a notebook.

You do not have to buy a fancy "Wine Record Card". Just purchase a small, plain notebook and keep it handy. When you make a new wine jot down the salient facts:

A2   ELDERBERRY   SW.

21.1.85   1 gal

    $2\frac{1}{2}$ lb elderberries (class 1)
    2 ripe bananas
    3 lb sugar
    2 tsp citric acid
    1 tsp nutrients
    1 vit B tablet
    C.W.E. yeast

If you wish you can make your notes of hydrometer readings etc. on the same page:

```
10.4.85   SG  1.020
28.4.85   SG  1.000   4oz sugar added
25.5.85   SG  1.010
29.6.85   SG  1.010   Filtered and bottled
```

Subsequently, when you try a bottle, you can make a brief note of your appreciation – "Needs more body. Increase bananas next time or try ½ pint port grape concentrate" or "Entered in village show 1987 – second prize. Repeat, but only with best quality elderberries." Do not ever open a bottle of wine from your cupboard for someone to admire and enjoy when you have only a vague memory of what went into it.

It is surprising what ideas, even inspiration, can come to you for variations on recipes when you skim back through old notebooks. Certainly it is silly to arrive at the blackberry season without being able to check on your good, and less good, experiences of making blackberry wine in previous years.

Should you find yourself with a stuck fermentatin or a particularly disappointing wine, look critically at your note of the recipe you used and try to discover the reasons. As for every other pursuit, experience is the key to success in winemaking. A notebook, rather than a vague memory, is the starting point.

Using a Home Computer

The most basic of home computers gives you the facility to store a programme on tape which can perform the same function as a notebook. My crude attempts with a ZX 81 (16K) prove that it must be easy!

```
10 PRINT "WINE 1985"
20 PRINT " "
30 PRINT "INDEX"
40 PRINT " "
50 PRINT "A1 BLACKBERRY    300"
60 PRINT "A2 ELDERBERRY    500"
```

and so on through your list of wines with sufficient spare lines at the end (up to line 290) to add new items.

The above index, which will appear when you LOAD and RUN "Wine 1985", will lead you to the individual reference of any particular wine you wish to put on the screen. You have 20 lines for each, on which you can enter code number and title, date and quantity, a list of ingredients and subsequently add in hydrometer readings and any comments or even show results. The only limit is the RAM facility available to you and the only risk is that you could erase the whole of your information accidentally – always keep a spare copy.

More sophisticated programmes can be written which will analyse aspects of a wine – alcohol level, acidity level, length of fermentation, and much more. No doubt such matters are under investigation elsewhere. For those of us who content ourselves with a limited understanding of the micro-chip there can remain a sense of fun in listing and recording our everyday winemaking data. But let's not forget that at this level it is only a substitute for the good old notebook.

CHAPTER 9

The First Division

All recipes are for one gallon.

Bilberry
Bilberries are an aristocratic fruit, somewhat elusive and slow in the picking but excellent for wines, particularly dry. If your back aches and your bag fills only gradually with bilberries you will almost certainly be on a beautiful hillside, made even more so by the contemplation of a glass of bilberry wine.

Sweet:
2½–3 lbs (1125–1350g) bilberries
liquor from 2 ripe bananas
3 lbs (1350g) sugar
1 tsp nutrients
1 vit B tablet
C.W.E. Formula 67 (or Port) yeast

Dry:
2 lbs (900g) bilberries
2½ lbs (1125g) sugar
1 tsp nutrients
1 vit B tablet
C.W.E. Formula 67 (or Burgundy) yeast

Method:
Normal pulp fermentation, as described in the previous chapter.

Bilberries are full of flavour and body in themselves, but if you insist upon incorporating grape juice into your recipe do so at the rate of half a pint of quality red concentrate per gallon. To compensate for this, reduce your fruit by 4 oz (110g) and the sugar by the same amount.

Blackberry

Many ordinary and disappointing wines are made from this plentiful fruit. The main problems are high acidity in dry wines and lack of body in the must for sweet wines. Once these inherent difficulties are overcome, however, the blackberry can produce superb results. It has that individual blue tinge to its redness in the glass which makes it unique.

As a generalisation, cultivated blackberries seem to make better wine than their hedgerow cousins. Nevertheless, providing that you are careful not to pick under-ripe berries, you can also achieve delightful results from wild blackberries.

Sweet:
3 lbs (1350g) blackberries
liquor from 4 ripe or dried bananas
½ lb (225g) chopped raisins or sultanas
3 lbs (1350g) sugar
1 tsp nutrients
1 vit B tablet
C.W.E. Formula 67 (or Port) yeast)

Dry:
2–2½ lbs (900–1125g) blackberries
2½ lbs (1125g) sugar
1 tsp nutrients
1 vit B tablet
C.W.E. Formula 67 (or Pommard) yeast

Method:
Normal pulp fermentation, but for dry wines strain off the pulp

after 3–5 days maximum and press fruit only lightly. Make an acid test (see Chapter 15) either by taste or a more precise method and adjust by gradual addition of acid reducing liquid, if necessary.

Blackberries are particularly useful for mixing with other fruits and several recipes are suggested later.

Cherry

Cherries make a good sweet dessert wine which is familiar in commercial form and a delicate dry wine which is not. Either Morello or black cherries can be used and the only important difference from our point of view is that you will have to add some acid if you are using black dessert types.

The main problem is the stones. If you mash your fruit and leave the stones in you will run the risk of an almondy flavour. Take great care not to break the stones when mashing. Ideally, get your hands wet and sticky when preparing cherry wine – pulp the fruit by hand and remove as many stones as possible.

Sweet:
   3 lbs (1350g) cherries
   3 lbs (1350g) sugar
   1 tsp citric or citric/tartaric acid if using black cherries
   1 tsp nutrients
   1 vit B tablet
   C.W.E. Formula 67 (or General Purpose) yeast

Dry:
   2½ lbs (1125g) cherries
   2½ lbs (1125g) sugar
   1 tsp citric or citric/tartaric acid if using black cherries
   1 tsp nutrients
   1 vit B tablet
   C.W.E. Formula 67 (or General Purpose) yeast

Method:
Normal pulp fermentation. If you have removed most of the stones,

Blackberries can make delicious and inexpensive wines and also mix well.

ferment for 5–7 days and press well on straining. Otherwise, 3 days will be sufficient and press only lightly. The acidity level of cherries varies, so make a check at some stage despite the efforts of the recipe.

Damson

This is an old favourite. A good year will bring a glut of damsons but do not be tempted to use in excess of 3 lbs (1350) per gallon. Generally fruit which makes good jam is likely to have a high proportion of pectin content and this is the case with damsons. Pectin will cause stubborn hazes. The recipe caters for it by the inclusion of a pectin-destroying enzyme.

Sweet:
3 lbs (1350g) damsons
liquor from 3 ripe bananas (optional)
3 lbs (1350g) sugar
2 tsp pectolase

1 tsp nutrients
1 vit B tablet
C.W.E. Formula 67 (or General Purpose) yeast

Do not bother with dry damson.

Method:
Normal pulp fermentation, but again we have the problem of the stones. Either mash by hand, remove the stones and ferment for 5–7 days or (less satisfactory) break the skins of the fruit and ferment on the pulp for only 3 or 4 days.

Dewberry

This unusual fruit is well worth searching out. A member of the blackberry family, it grows low to the ground on sandy stretches near to the coast. The fruit itself has a greyish bloom and is far superior to the blackberry. A good dry dewberry will win prizes for you whereas another pound of berries can enable you to make a rich dessert wine, if you prefer it. Dewberries ripen more evenly than the blackberry and seem to have a better balance, particularly with regard to acid content.

Sweet:
3–3$\frac{1}{2}$ lbs (1350–1600g) dewberries
liquor from 2 or 3 ripe bananas
3 lbs (1350g) sugar
1 tsp nutrients
1 vit B tablet
C.W.E. Formula 67 (or Port) yeast

Dry:
2$\frac{1}{2}$ lbs (1125g) dewberries
2$\frac{1}{2}$ lb (1125g) sugar
1 tsp nutrients
1 vit B tablet
C.W.E. Formula 67 (or Pommard) yeast

Method:
Normal pulp fermentation.

Elderberry

"The Englishman's grape" is an abundant berry which you need to share with no jam or pastry makers. Only the birds and the winemaker are at all interested.

Many newly interested winemakers rush out and pick elderberries, make a gallon of "port" and are sadly disappointed. Elderberry is never a quick wine. The high tannin content makes it harsh in its youth and you require patience to produce that smooth, heady wine which so many can recall from their past.

There are ways of lessening the force of the tannin and the incorporation of a starch element into the must can help. To this end the liquor from a boil of young runner beans can be used. Do not use old, stringy beans and, above all, do not use the water from beans you have boiled for a meal – it will have salt in it. Try runners occasionally in your sweet elderberry wine – do not use them always.

Sweet:
  2½ lbs (1125g) elderberries
  liquor from 4 ripe or dried bananas
  ½ lb (225g) chopped sultanas (optional)
  liquor from 1 lb (450g) runner beans (optional)
  3 lbs (1350g) sugar
  1½ tsp citric or citric/tartaric acid
  1 tsp nutrients
  1 vit B tablet
  C.W.E. Formula 67 (or Port) yeast

Dry:
Elderberries do not readily lend themselves to a dry wine and it is a true test of skill to produce a good dry elderberry. You must have patience and look towards maturing for years rather than months. Fining with a lightly whipped egg white will reduce the tannin content a little before bottling.

Dry:

1¾ lbs (800g) elderberries
½ lb (225g) sultanas (chopped)
2½ lbs (1125g) sugar
1 tsp citric or citric/tartaric acid
1 tsp nutrients
1 vit B tablet
C.W.E. Formula 67 (or General Purpose) yeast

Method:

Normal pulp fermentation. Make sure that the berries are ripe – beginning to hang and full of juice, rather than just red. Strip them from the stalks with a fork or by hand.

Elderberries give opportunities for mixing with other fruits. Some examples are given later and many more can be found in "Winemaking with Elderberries" by T. Edwin Belt.

Ginger

Ginger wine is hardly British, hardly a wine at all, and yet it merits a place in the First Division. For one thing it can be made in the winter, when there are only citrus fruits and the remnants in the freezer to occupy the winemaker. More importantly, it is possible to produce a ginger wine at least on a par with those sold commercially and it makes a welcome change from fruit wine on a cold winter's evening.

Ginger in itself will not ferment – it is a root spice. What we do is to concoct a fruit base from either sultanas or grape concentrate. Use root ginger, not powdered ginger. Most recipes do not include enough ginger to give that distinctive tang that makes the wine so individual.

Sweet:

4 oz (110g) root ginger
1 lb (450g) chopped sultanas (or 1 pint (½ litre) of grape concentrate)
2¾ lbs (1250g) sugar
(2 lbs (900g) if using grape conc.)

1½ tsp citric or citric/tartaric acid
1 tsp nutrients
1 vit B tablet
C.W.E. Formula 67 (or General Purpose) yeast

Special Method:
Break the root pieces into smaller strips or chunks, so that the
inner fibres are exposed. This is done most easily with conventional
nut crackers or by rolling the root in a clean towel and applying a
light hammer. Chop or mince the sultanas and mix into the must
for a normal pulp fermentation of about 7 days.

Before you bottle your wine check whether the ginger flavour is
sufficiently strong for your palate. If not, break up another ounce
or two of ginger root, wrap in a piece of muslin and suspend in
your wine for ten days or a fortnight.

Be careful that before you make your next wine your fermentation bucket has been particularly well cleaned – otherwise there
may be a gingery taste to be picked up by the next fermentation.

Gooseberry

The main thing to remember with gooseberries is that ripe ones
do not give particularly good results. Especially for dry wines, you
need gooseberries which have been picked green.

Gooseberries   *E. L. Tombs*

Sweet:
   $3\frac{1}{2}$ lbs (1600g) gooseberries (can be all ripe but a proportion of
      about a third green is best)
   liquor from 3 ripe bananas
   3 lbs (1350g) sugar
   1 tsp nutrients
   1 vit B tablet
   C.W.E. Formula 67 (or Sauternes) yeast

Dry:
   $2\frac{1}{2}$ lbs (1125g) green gooseberries
   $\frac{1}{2}$ lb (225g) chopped sultanas
   liquor from 1 ripe banana
   $2\frac{1}{2}$ lbs (1125g) sugar
   1 tsp nutrients
   1 vit B tablet
   C.W.E. Formula 67 (or Chablis) yeast

Method:
Normal pulp fermentation, except that your green gooseberries
will not mash. You will need either to chop or mince them.

Grapefruit

Grapefruit and orange can make excellent wines, but there seems
to be a great variation in results. The fruit needs to be very ripe –
almost invariably you will need to ripen on before using them.
Place the newly purchased grapefruit in a warm place until it begins
to show an orange tinge rather than the light yellow of the
greengrocer's shelf.

There are three basic problems with citric wines, but they can
be overcome with a little care. Firstly, the fruit lacks body. We
have the alternatives of bananas or sultanas or grape concentrate
to deal with this. Secondly, the zest of the fruit contains the real
flavour, but we must be careful not to overdo this and, most
importantly, not to include any of the white pith (which is bitter).
Thirdly, there is the obvious possibility of an over-acid wine and
some adjustment may be necessary before bottling.

Great skill is necessary to be able to produce a good dry wine from any citrus fruit. Grapefruit are better suited to sweet.

Sweet:
  8 ripe grapefruit
  liquor from 4 ripe bananas
  $\frac{3}{4}$ lb (350g) chopped sultanas
  3 lbs (1350g) sugar
  $\frac{1}{4}$ tsp grape tannin
  1 tsp nutrients
  1 vit B tablet
  C.W.E. Formula 67 (or General Purpose) yeast

Dry:
  6 ripe grapefruit
  liquor from 1 ripe banana
  $\frac{1}{2}$ lb (225g) chopped sultanas
  $2\frac{1}{2}$ lbs (1125g) sugar
  $\frac{1}{4}$ tsp grape tannin
  1 tsp nutrients
  1 vit B tablet
  C.W.E. Formula 67 (or General Purpose) yeast

Special Method:
Thinly pare the zest from one grapefruit (choosing a clean and unmottled fruit) with either a cheese grater or apple peeler. Make sure that no white pith is attached. Cut all of the fruit into halves and extract the juice with a lemon squeezer. Strain and press this so that no pips or flesh are included in the must. Cut or chop the sultanas so that your must consists of zest, juice and sultanas – over this you pour the hot liquors and proceed as for a normal pulp fermentation.

Before bottling make an acid check and adjustment. The various ways of doing this are discussed in detail later. However, bear in mind that an over-adjustment will leave you with a bland wine – you are aiming at a slightly acid tang, in character with the style of wine which you have made.

Loganberry

Generally superior to wild blackberries and at least on a par with cultivated, the loganberry is underestimated by many as a winemaking fruit. It is a cross between raspberry and blackberry and there are several other crosses with fancy names, such as Marionberry, which you can grow in the garden and substitute for the more familiar loganberry.

Make sure that the loganberries are ripe – this is a factor which the birds will recognise before you, so net the fruit before they turn black.

Sweet:
   3 lbs (1350g) loganberries
   liquor from 2–3 ripe bananas
   3 lbs (1350g) sugar
   1 tsp nutrients
   1 vit B tablet
   C.W.E. Formula 67 (or Port) yeast

Dry:
   2–2½ lbs (900–1125g) loganberries
   ½ lb (225g) chopped sultanas (optional)
   liquor from 1 ripe banana
   2½ lbs (1125g) sugar
   1 tsp nutrients
   1 vit B tablet
   C.W.E. Formula 67 (or Pommard) yeast

Method:
Normal pulp fermentation. Particularly with the dry wine, make an acid check and adjustment before bottling. If your garden produces loganberries, but not in sufficient quantities for a gallon of wine, bear in mind that they mix well with other ingredients.

Orange

Oranges can make a fine wine. Like grapefruit they are available all year round and therefore invaluable in winter months.

The problems are the same as for grapefruit with the additional complication of a bewildering choice of types. Your objective should be sweet, juicy oranges, not necessarily large ones. Jaffa types can make excellent wines, but generally the smaller varieties are to be preferred. Navels are good: what we used as children to call "blood oranges" are even better. Ripen on your fruit for about a week unless they are remarkably ripe when you buy them.

Sweet:
   20–25 small to medium sized sweet oranges
   $\frac{1}{2}$ lb (225g) chopped sultanas
   liquor from 1 ripe banana
   $2\frac{3}{4}$ lbs (1250g) sugar ($2\frac{1}{2}$ lbs (1125g) if the oranges are very ripe)
   $\frac{1}{4}$ tsp grape tannin
   1 tsp nutrients
   1 vit B tablet
   C.W.E. Formula 67 (or General Purpose) yeast

Dry:
   15 small to medium sized sweet oranges
   $\frac{1}{2}$ lb (225g) chopped sultanas
   $2\frac{1}{4}$–$2\frac{1}{2}$ lbs (800–900g) sugar
   $\frac{1}{4}$ tsp grape tannin
   1 tsp nutrients
   1 vit B tablet
   C.W.E. Formula 67 (or Chablis) yeast

Special Method:
As for grapefruit. Include the finely pared zest of 3 oranges for the sweet wine but only 1 for the dry, again choosing sound fruit. Check and adjust the acidity before bottling, but do not make the wine bland or it will lose its character.

Peach
   If your peaches are ripe enough, you can make a good sweet, rich wine. The most economical way to obtain them, particularly

in a hot summer, is to cash in on the fact that peaches have a short "shelf" life. Ask your greengrocer if he has any over-ripe peaches for winemaking. The chances are that he will produce a tray or two of fruit which has the odd bruise or patch of mould which can be cut away to leave plenty of succulent flesh for your bucket. You will have to pay, but not to the same extent as a purchase of sound peaches. If you do not have a friendly greengrocer, wait until prices are at their lowest and buy in bulk – you can freeze any surplus.

Peaches *must* be ripe or you will have a nasty "green" tasting end-product. Reject any sign of hardness in the flesh and put that fruit aside to ripen on – if the majority of your peaches are not soft to the touch leave them a few days. There is a considerable pectin problem with peaches, but we can overcome that.

Sweet:
   2½–3 lbs (1125–1350g) ripe peach pulp
   3 lbs (1350g) sugar
   3 tsp pectolase
   ¼ tsp grape tannin
   1 tsp nutrients
   1 vit B tablet
   C.W.E. Formula 67 (or General Purpose) yeast

Special Method:
Unless you are prepared to skin your peaches, and particularly in cases where mould or bad bruises are being cut away from the fruit, a sulphiting method is advisable.

Cut away bad and marked parts of the peaches, wash and chop away from stones (which should be discarded). Pulp the flesh in the bucket, cover with cold water and stir in the pectolase. Dissolve one Campden tablet in warm (not hot) water and stir this in also. Cover and leave 12–24 hours. Proceed as for normal pulp fermentation, except that the liquors should be cooled before adding into the must.

Rhubarb

Considered by many a second-rate fruit, rhubarb has a place in the upper rank of wines if you follow the special method below.

It produces a light, fresh wine without excessive acid.

It is the excess of oxalic acid which has given winemakers so much trouble over the years. You will even see recipes which include precipitated chalk to neutralise this acid. There is no need to go to these lengths if you restrict the extraction of juices to reasonable proportions.

Sweet:
    3 lbs (1350g) young rhubarb
    liquor of 1 ripe banana
    3 lbs (1350g) sugar
    $\frac{1}{4}$ tsp grape tannin
    1 tsp pectolase
    1 tsp nutrients
    1 vit B tablet
    C.W.E. Formula 67 (or General Purpose) yeast

Special Method:
This method uses the sugar to draw the flavour out of the rhubarb without creating acidity problems. The fermentation bucket is used to extract the flavour before the yeast is introduced.

Chop the sticks into $\frac{1}{2}$–1 inch (2–3cm) pieces. Liquefy the sugar in enough hot water to give about four pints of syrup. Place the rhubarb in the fermentation bucket either in layers or shaken down in a fairly level way. Dissolve one Campden tablet in warm water and mix thoroughly into the syrup. Pour this over the rhubarb. If all of the fruit is not covered add the necessary amount of cold water and stir in. Cover tightly and place in a cool spot for 2 or 3 days. Remove all rhubarb pieces from the liquid, washing any excess sugar from the rhubarb by rinsing back into the bucket. Add the remaining ingredients, stir well and strain directly into the gallon jar. Remember that the initial fermentation may well be violent and you will need at least a 3 inch (7$\frac{1}{2}$cm) air gap at the top of the demijohn (this can be reduced by topping up with cold water at first racking). Fit an airlock and ferment on.

There should be no need for an acid adjustment with this method. The last thing you want is an insipid, neutralised rhubarb wine.

CHAPTER 10

The Second Division

The fruits in this division are marginally less attractive than those in the first division with two exceptions. In the cases of apple and birch sap I have relegated them because of practical difficulties rather than any individual lack of potential.

Apple

The problem with apples lies in extracting the juice. Beware of any recipe which advocates chopping the apples into chunks and fermenting these chunks as pulp – your chances of a decent wine are minimal. Mincing or grating the apples is better, but rarely very successful.

A cider press, juice extractor or a liquidiser attachment to a kitchen blender is necessary to break down the fruit. For most winemakers, this means the last. It is a messy business to liquidise enough apples for a gallon, but the results can be good. Chop the apples, avoiding both cores and peel, and liquidise with as little water as is necessary until you have a gallon (or just over) of runny pulp.

The apples used should be a mix of dessert and cookers, even with a handful of crab apples for good measure, and you may need around 10 lbs (4500–5000g) in total.

Sweet:

8–10 pints (4.5–5.7 litres) of liquidised apples (or 6 pints (3.5 litres) of extracted juice)
liquor from 1 ripe banana
$\frac{1}{2}$ lb (225g) chopped sultanas
$2\frac{1}{2}$ lbs (1125g) sugar

$\frac{1}{4}$ tsp grape tannin
1 tsp pectolase
1 tsp nutrients
1 vit B tablet
C.W.E. Formula 67 (or Riesling) yeast

Dry:
6–7 pints (3.5–6–8 litres) of liquidised apples (or 5 pints (3 litres) of extracted juice)
liquor from 1 banana
$\frac{1}{2}$ lb (225g) chopped sultanas
2 lbs (900g) sugar
$\frac{1}{4}$ tsp grape tannin
1 tsp pectolase
1 tsp nutrients
1 vit B tablet
C.W.E. Formula 67 (or Chablis) yeast

Special Method:
You can sulphite if you wish, leaving the pulp for a few hours. Ferment in a bucket for 5–7 days and carefully strain into the demijohn with a jug so that the very worst of the apple "sludge" remains in the bucket for disposal.

It will be at about the third racking that you begin to realise that you have a wine. At each racking leave the worst of the pulp (about 2 inches (5cm)) to be rinsed out of the jar – you can top up each time with cold water. Check and adjust the acidity before bottling.

Birch Sap

Why this is such a superb wine, I do not know. It is said that it was a Russian favourite over a hundred years ago and certainly it has a character all of its own.

The problem, of course, is getting a gallon of birch sap. It can only be taken during a few weeks of spring, when the sap is rising. The first warm spell in March/April is the likely time.

The tree has to be "tapped" and it must be of sufficient girth (at least 1 foot (30cm) across) to allow for the sap being taken without doing damage to the tree. The sap moves in the outer wood, inside the bark layer, so you will need some tools. Drill a $\frac{1}{2}$ inch (1–1$\frac{1}{2}$cm) diameter hole at 45° (upwards) into the tree about 2 feet (60cm) from the ground until sap trickles in the hole. You should not need to drill deeper than 2–2$\frac{1}{2}$ inches (5–7cm) or so. Push $\frac{1}{2}$ inch tubing into the hole and place a demijohn below with the other end of the tube in it. Seal round the neck of the jar with a plastic bag to keep out foreign bodies. You do this by slitting the bag just sufficiently for the tubing to pass through it – do not make an air-tight seal or you could create a vacuum.

The rate of flow varies, but you should collect a gallon in 12–24 hours. If the tree is not in your own garden, it will be quite exciting to return to the site, not knowing whether your jar has been stolen or overturned. It is amazing to see a gallon of clear sap – the jar looks empty from a distance.

One type of filter available as a kit makes use of crystals and powder for the filtration process. Check costs of refills of these items.

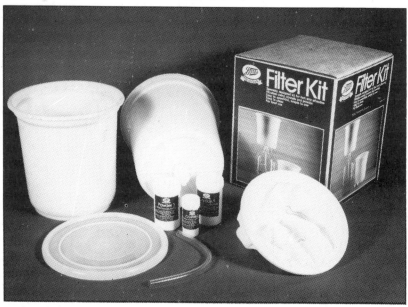

Do not just walk away from the tree with your spoils. The wound must be healed. Take a $\frac{3}{4}$ inch (2cm) long tapered dowel with you and hammer this into the hole carefully so that the sap no longer flows. Try a different tree the following year.

Birch sap is neither fermentable in itself nor does it have any real substance or flavour. Fruit has to be added in just the right minimal quantities to achieve the perfect wine.

Sweet:
1 gallon (5.7 litres) birch sap
liquor of 1 ripe banana
$\frac{1}{2}$ lb (225g) chopped sultanas
juice of 3 ripe oranges
$2\frac{3}{4}$ lbs (1250g) sugar
$\frac{3}{4}$ tsp grape tannin
$\frac{1}{2}$ tsp citric or citric/tartaric acid
1 tsp nutrients
1 vit B tablet
C.W.E. Formula 67 (or General Purpose) yeast

Method:
Boil the birch sap with the sugar for a few minutes, cool and proceed with a normal pulp fermentation for 5–7 days. No acid adjustments should be necessary, but be patient with this wine.

Blackcurrant
There are certain fruits, of which blackcurrants, strawberries and mulberries are examples, which have such a strong flavour that they do not easily lend themselves to wine. It is not difficult to end up with an alcoholic cordial which is totally without subtlety.

I have included blackcurrant because it is popular with some winemakers. Personally I would give the currants to someone who can make jam. If you have a glut, however, try this recipe:

Sweet:
2–$2\frac{1}{2}$ lbs (900–1125g) blackcurrants

liquor from 2 ripe bananas
½ lb (225g) chopped sultanas
2¾ lbs (1250g) sugar
1 tsp pectolase
1 tsp nutrients
1 vit B tablet
C.W.E. Formula 67 (or General Purpose) yeast

Method:
Normal pulp fermentation. There is no need to "top and tail" the currants before mashing them.

Dried Elderberry
Elderberries can be purchased in dried form. They are imported and their availability and cost varies from year to year. They make excellent wines. Dried elderberries do not have the high tannin content of fresh ones and you can produce a palatable wine far more quickly.

Sweet:
1 lb (450g) dried elderberries
liquor from 3–4 ripe bananas
3 lbs (1350g) sugar
1½ tsp citric/tartaric acid
1 tsp nutrients
1 vit B tablet
C.W.E. Formula 67 (or General Purpose) yeast

Dry:
¾ lb (350g) dried elderberries
liquor from 1–2 ripe bananas
2½ lbs (1125g) sugar
1 tsp citric or citric/tartaric acid
1 tsp nutrients
1 vit B tablet
C.W.E. Formula 67 (or General Purpose) yeast

Method:

Pour the hot liquors over the dried berries and do not bother to mash at this stage. Cool and proceed as for the normal pulp fermentation (5–7 days). Squeeze berries firmly with the back of a spoon when straining into the gallon jar.

Green Elderberry

Amongst the common elder bushes you will find the odd one where the berries remain green when they are ripe. These make a very different wine. Be careful, of course, that you are picking ripe green berries and not under-ripe red ones. The flavour is rather strong, so go easy on your fruit content.

Sweet:

$1\frac{1}{2}$–2 lbs (575–900g) green elderberries
$\frac{3}{4}$ lb (350g) chopped sultanas
liquor from 2 ripe bananas
$2\frac{3}{4}$ lbs (1250g) sugar
1 tsp citric or citric/tartaric acid
$\frac{3}{4}$ tsp grape tannin
1 tsp pectolase
1 tsp nutrients
1 vit B tablet
C.W.E. Formula 67 (or Sauternes) yeast

Dry:

$1\frac{1}{2}$ lbs (675g) max. green elderberries
$\frac{1}{2}$ lb (225g) chopped sultanas
liquor from 1 ripe banana
$2\frac{1}{2}$ lbs (1125g) sugar
$\frac{1}{2}$ tsp citric or citric/tartaric acid
$\frac{1}{4}$ tsp grape tannin
1 tsp pectolase
1 tsp nutrients
1 vit B tablet
C.W.E. Formula 67 (or Chablis) yeast

Method:
Normal pulp fermentation (5–7 days). The acidity level varies, so make a check.

Lemon

Lemons are rather less suitable for winemaking than oranges or grapefruit, but do try them. Make sure the lemons are very ripe – in fact, put your fruit in a warm place until they are as ripe as you can get them without the skins turning brown.

Sweet:
>**12 fair sized lemons**
>**$\frac{1}{2}$ lb (225g) chopped sultanas**
>**liquor from 1 ripe banana**
>**3 lbs (1350g) sugar**
>**$\frac{3}{4}$ tsp grape tannin**
>**1 tsp nutrients**
>**1 vit B tablet**
>**C.W.E. Formula 67 (or Sauternes) yeast**

Dry:
>**8 fair sized lemons**
>**$\frac{1}{2}$ lb (225g) chopped sultanas**
>**$2\frac{1}{2}$ lbs (1125g) sugar**
>**$\frac{1}{4}$ tsp grape tannin**
>**1 tsp nutrients**
>**1 vit B tablet**
>**C.W.E. Formula 67 (or Chablis) yeast**

Method:
Thinly pare the rind from one quality lemon for the sweet wine or half a lemon for the dry wine. Extract the juice with a lemon squeezer. Mix peel, strained juice and sultanas in the fermenting bucket and proceed as normal. An acid check is essential. Your aim should be to leave a subtle tang of lemon rather than any overpowering acidity.

Pineapple
Again, the fruit must be very ripe to make a good wine.

Sweet:
2 large pineapples
½ lb (225g) chopped sultanas
liquor from 2–3 ripe bananas
3 lbs (1350g) sugar
¾ tsp tannin
1 tsp pectolase
1 tsp nutrients
1 vit B tablet
C.W.E. Formula 67 (or General Purpose) yeast

Dry:
2 medium pineapples
liquor from 1 ripe banana
2½ lbs (1125g) sugar
¾ tsp tannin
1 tsp pectolase
1 tsp nutrients
1 vit B tablet
C.W.E. Formula 67 (or General Purpose) yeast

Method:
Remove the skin from the fruit and chop the flesh into small chunks. Press the pulp as much as possible. Ferment on the pulp for 3–5 days only. An acid adjustment will almost certainly be necessary.

Plum
Plum wine is not to everyone's taste and I would avoid dry plum unless you have a glut and hate sweet wines. Victorias are not as good as red plums, but better than yellow ones. The fruit must be very ripe.

Sweet:

 $3\frac{1}{2}$ **lbs (1600g) plums**
 3 lbs (1350g) sugar
 3 tsp pectolase
 $\frac{3}{4}$ **tsp grape tannin**
 1 tsp nutrients
 1 vit B tablet
 C.W.E. Formula 67 (or General Purpose) yeast

Dry:

 $2-2\frac{1}{2}$ **lbs (900–1125g) plums**
 $\frac{1}{2}$ **lb (225g) chopped sultanas**
 $2\frac{1}{2}$ **lbs (1125g) sugar**
 2 tsp pectolase
 $\frac{1}{4}$ **tsp grape tannin**
 1 tsp nutrients
 1 vit B tablet
 C.W.E. Formula 67 (or General Purpose) yeast

Method:

Remove the stones from the plums before proceeding with a normal pulp fermentation (5–7 days).

Pomegranate

 A distinctive sweet wine can be made from pomegranates. It will not win any prizes for you but it is pleasantly different.

Sweet:

 8 pomegranates
 $\frac{1}{2}$ **lb (225g) chopped sultanas**
 liquor from 2 ripe bananas
 3 lbs (1350g) sugar
 $\frac{1}{4}$ **tsp grape tannin**
 1 tsp nutrients
 1 vit B tablet
 C.W.E. Formula 67 (or General Purpose) yeast

Method:
Scoop the inside of the pomegranates into a bowl, discarding all trace of the yellow pith membranes. Crush the fruit, strain and throw away the pips, so that you have only the liquid left. Proceed as for normal fermentation – you can go directly to the demijohn if you wish, the only solids being the sultanas.

If you want a rosé, cover the jar or use coloured glass.

Raspberry

This is another distinctive wine which is much adored, especially by the ladies. The fruit makes a good sweet, social wine, rather than a wine you would drink with dinner. Do not attempt a dry wine – the flavour is wrong. Raspberries almost invariably ferment at a hectic pace and the wine drops clear very readily.

Sweet:
$2\frac{1}{2}$ lbs (1125g) raspberries
liquor from 2 ripe bananas
3 lbs (1350g) sugar
$\frac{1}{4}$ tsp grape tannin
1 tsp nutrients
1 vit B tablet
C.W.E. Formula 67 (or General purpose) yeast

Method:
Normal pulp fermentation. The acid level should be acceptable providing that your raspberries were fully ripe.

Redcurrant

Whereas blackcurrants have an over-abundance of flavour, redcurrants tend to produce a rather "thin" wine which lacks character. Sultanas and bananas help us to give some shape to the wine. Concentrate upon sweet wines if you have a limited supply of the fruit.

Sweet:
$3-3\frac{1}{2}$ lbs (1350–1600g) redcurrants

$\frac{3}{4}$ lb (350g) chopped sultanas
liquor from 3–4 ripe bananas
2$\frac{3}{4}$ lbs (1250g) sugar
$\frac{1}{4}$ tsp grape tannin
1 tsp nutrients
1 vit B tablet
C.W.E. Formula 67 (or General Purpose) yeast

Dry:
2$\frac{3}{4}$–3 lbs (1250–1350g) redcurrants
$\frac{1}{2}$ lb (225g) chopped sultanas
liquor from 1 ripe banana
2$\frac{3}{4}$ lbs (1000g) sugar
$\frac{1}{4}$ tsp grape tannin
1 tsp nutrients
1 vit B tablet
C.W.E. Formula 67 (or General Purpose) yeast

Method:
Normal pulp fermentation with an acid check either at "must" or bottling stage.

Rosehip

A very late autumn wine is a useful addition to our range, but results can vary tremendously. At its best rosehip wine is reckoned by some to be second only to the grape. This is probably an exaggeration.

Pick rosehips late, just before the birds, because you want them soft and sticky rather than hard and pleasant.

Sweet:
3$\frac{1}{2}$ lbs (1600g) rosehips
liquor from 3 ripe bananas
1 tsp pectolase
$\frac{1}{4}$ tsp grape tannin
3 lbs (1350g) sugar

1 tsp nutrients
1 vit B tablet
any sweet white wine yeast culture (e.g. Sauternes)

Dry:
    2½ lbs (1125g) rosehips
    liquor from 1 ripe banana
    1 tsp pectolase
    ¼ tsp grape tannin
    2½ lbs (1125g) sugar
    1 tsp nutrients
    1 vit B tablet
    any dry white wine yeast culture (e.g. Chablis)

Method:
Either mince or (preferably) liquidise your rosehips after washing them well. Proceed as for a normal pulp fermentation. Rosehips are said, at their best, to take on the characteristics of a particular yeast culture, so it is as well to use a named yeast type.

Make an acid check before bottling and adjust, as necessary, either way.

Sloe

In an ideal world every sloe that ripens would find itself used for sloe gin. This is an old favourite which is splendid. In fact, of course, sloe gin is not a wine – it is a mock liqueur. There is no yeast and no fermentation involved in its production. Nevertheless, one cannot pass over sloes without giving a recipe for this nectar.

The following will provide you with a bottle – in fact, slightly more than a bottle due to the sugar.

Sloe Gin:
    1 lb (450g) sloes
    10 oz (275g) sugar
    1 bottle of gin (it does not have to be the most expensive)

Method:
Wash sloes. Prick them with a needle as many times as your patience will allow and drop them into a demijohn. Pour the sugar over them without bothering to make a syrup of it, followed by the gin. Fit a solid bung, give a swirl and place in a dark cupboard. Leave for 2–3 months, occasionally swirling the contents. Sieve the liquid from the sloes and filter it. Put away to mature.

A sloe gin made in the autumn will be drinkable by Christmas, absolute nectar by the following Christmas.

Sloe Wine
Sloes are by no means as suitable for wine, but they make a reasonable sweet rosé:

3 lbs (1350g) sloes
liquor from 3 ripe bananas
3 lbs (1350g) sugar
1 tsp nutrients
1 vit B tablet
C.W.E. Formula 67 (or General Purpose) yeast

Method:
Mash the sloes without trying to remove the stones. Use a normal pulp fermentation (5–7 days) with an acid check.

Tangerine
Various delicate wines can be made from tangerines, satsumas, clementines and the like. They must be ripe.

Sweet:
4 lbs (1800g) tangerines
$\frac{1}{2}$ lb (225g) chopped sultanas
liquor from 1 ripe banana
$2\frac{3}{4}$ lbs (1250g) sugar
$\frac{1}{4}$ tsp grape tannin
1 tsp nutrients

72

1 vit B tablet
C.W.E. Formula 67 (or General Purpose) yeast

Dry:
   3 lbs (1350g) tangerines
   $\frac{1}{2}$ lb (225g) chopped sultanas
   $2\frac{1}{2}$ lbs (1125g) sugar
   $\frac{1}{4}$ tsp grape tannin
   1 tsp nutrients
   1 vit B tablet
   C.W.E. Formula 67 (or General Purpose) yeast

Method:
Sweet wine: include the finely pared zest of 2 sound fruit. Avoid the pith. Use a lemon squeezer to extract the juice and put this through a sieve. Dry wine: use the juice only. The acid level will require a careful check before you bottle.

Elderberries, partially ripened, usually plentiful in August.

73

CHAPTER 11

Mixing Reliable Ingredients

Some winemaking ingredients make better wines when used in a mix with others than they do on their own. We have established that bananas and sultanas certainly do. If you must use parsnips, hide them in a mixed wine.

At the risk of upsetting diehards, I reckon that elderberries are better when their harshness is mitigated in a mixed wine. There is more chance of producing a good sweet elderberry and blackberry than a good sweet elderberry.

Port Style

Most winemakers try their hand at a rich port type wine from odds and ends of autumn or from the freezer. As a general rule, anything over 4 lbs (1800g) of red fruit in a must is a recipe for disappointment. However, given a careful check on the final acidity level, a degree of patience in allowing the heavy wine to mature can be rewarded. Try one of the following:

Port Style 1
    2 lbs (900g) bilberries
    2 lbs (900g) loganberries (or cultivated blackberries)
    1 lb (450g) black cherries
    liquor from 3–4 ripe bananas
    3 lbs (1350g) sugar
    2 tsp pectolase
    1 tsp nutrients
    1 vit B tablet
    Port yeast culture

Port Style 2

1½ lbs (675g) blackberries
1 lb (450g) elderberries
½ lb (225) raspberries
1 lb (450g) bilberries (or sloes)
liquor from 3 ripe bananas
3 lbs (1350g) sugar
2 tsp pectolase
1 tsp nutrients
1 vit B tablet
Port yeast culture

Port Style 3

2 lbs (900g) blackberries
1½ lbs (675g) elderberries
1 lb (450g) sloes
1 lb (450g) redcurrants
1 lb (450g) chopped raisins
3 lbs (1350g) sugar
2 tsp pectolase
1 tsp nutrients
1 vit B tablet
Port yeast culture

Method:
Normal pulp fermentation, with only light pressing on straining into the demijohn. These rich, heavy wines are usually over-acid, but bear in mind that a full-bodied wine will stand a higher level of acidity than a normal one. Mature for at least one year, preferably three.

Established Favourites

The following mixes are well known to winemakers as producing excellent wines from common fruits:

75

Apple and Gooseberry

Sweet:

   4 pints (2.25 litres) of liquidised mixed apples (or 3 pints (1.75
      litres) of extracted juice)
   2 lbs (900g) gooseberries (including a proportion under-ripe)
   liquor from 2 ripe bananas
   $2\frac{3}{4}$ lbs (1250g) sugar
   1 tsp pectolase
   $\frac{1}{4}$ tsp grape tannin
   1 tsp nutrients
   1 vit B tablet
   C.W.E. Formula 67 (or Hock) yeast

Dry:

   3 pints (1.75 litres) mixed apples (or $2\frac{1}{2}$ pints (1.5 litres) extracted
      juice)
   $1\frac{1}{2}$ lbs (675g) green gooseberries
   liquor from 1 ripe banana
   $2\frac{1}{2}$ lbs (1125g) sugar
   1 tsp pectolase
   $\frac{1}{4}$ tsp grape tannin
   1 tsp nutrients
   1 vit B tablet
   C.W.E. Formula 67 (or Chablis yeast)

Method:
The green gooseberries will require chopping or mincing. Otherwise
proceed as normal. An acid test will be essential.

Blackberry and Apple

Sweet:

   2 lbs (900g) blackberries
   4 pints (2.25 litres) of liquidised mixed apples (or 3 pints (1.75
      litres) of extracted juice)

liquor from 2 ripe bananas
2¾ lbs (1250g) sugar
1 tsp pectolase
1 tsp nutrients
1 vit B tablet
C.W.E. Formula 67 (or General Purpose) yeast

Dry:
1½ lbs (675g) blackberries
3 pints (1.75 litres) of liquidised dessert apples (or 2½ pints (1.5
   litres) of extracted juice)
½ lb (225g) chopped sultanas
2½ lbs (1125g) sugar
1 tsp pectolase
1 tsp nutrients
1 vit B tablet
C.W.E. Formula 67 (or General Purpose) yeast

Method:
Normal pulp fermentation with a careful acid check either in the
initial stages or before bottling.

Elderberry and Blackberry

Sweet:
1½ lbs (675g) elderberries
1½–2 lbs (675–900g) blackberries
liquor from 3 ripe bananas
3 lbs(1350g) sugar
1 tsp nutrients
1 vit B tablet
C.W.E. Formula 67 (or Port) yeast

Dry:
¾ lb (375g) elderberries
1½ lbs (675g) blackberries

$\frac{1}{2}$ lb (225g) chopped sultanas
2$\frac{1}{2}$ lbs (1125g) sugar
1 tsp nutrients
1 vit B tablet
C.W.E. Formula 67 (or Pommard) yeast

Method:
Normal method with an acid test. The dry wine, in particular, will require maturing.

Dried Elderberry and Blackberry

Sweet:
$\frac{1}{2}$ lb(225g) dried elderberries
2 lbs (900g) blackberries
liquor from 3 ripe bananas
3 lbs (1350g) sugar
1 tsp nutrients
1 vit B tablet
C.W.E. Formula 67 (or General Purpose) yeast

Dry:
$\frac{1}{2}$ lb (225g) dried elderberries
1$\frac{1}{4}$ lbs (1000g) blackberries
liquor from 1 ripe banana
2$\frac{1}{2}$ lbs (1125g) sugar
1 tsp nutrients
1 vit B tablet
C.W.E. Formula 67 (or General Purpose) yeast

Method:
Pour boiling water over elderberries before you liquefy the sugar, then proceed normally. You should only need to adjust the acid if you have used hedgerow blackberries. This wine can be drunk young, if you are the impatient type.

Redcurrant and Blackcurrant

Neither fruit is particularly good in itself, but each benefits from mixing. The recipe also suits many people with a small fruit garden.

Sweet:

2 lbs (900g) redcurrants
1 lb (450g) blackcurrants
liquor from 2 ripe bananas
3 lbs (1350g) sugar
1 tsp nutrients
1 vit B tablet
C.W.E. Formula 67 (or General Purpose) yeast

Method:

Normal pulp fermentation. Adjust the acidity at some stage.

Less Familiar Mixes

Bilberry and Blackberry

Sweet:

1½ lbs (675g) bilberries
2 lbs (900g) cultivated blackberries
liquor from 3 ripe bananas
3 lbs (1350g) sugar
1 tsp nutrients
1 vit B tablet
C.W.E. Formula 67 (or Port) yeast

Dry:

1¼ lbs (550g) bilberries
1 lb (450g) cultivated blackberries
2½ lbs (1125g) sugar
1 tsp nutrients
1 vit B tablet
C.W.E. Formula 67 (or Bordeaux) yeast

Method:
Normal pulp fermentation with an acid check.

Bilberry and Loganberry

Sweet:
   $1\frac{1}{2}$ lbs (675g) bilberries
   $1\frac{1}{2}$ lbs (675g) loganberries
   liquor from 2 ripe bananas
   3 lbs (1350g) sugar
   1 tsp nutrients
   1 vit B tablet
   C.W.E. Formula 67 (or Port) yeast

Dry:
   $1\frac{1}{4}$ lbs (550g) bilberries
   1 lb (450g) loganberries
   $2\frac{1}{2}$ lbs (1125g) sugar
   1 tsp nutrients
   1 vit B tablet
   C.W.E. Formula 67 (or Bordeaux) yeast

Method:
Normal pulp fermentation with an acid check.

Bilberry and Peach

Sweet:
   2 lbs (900g) bilberries
   $1\frac{1}{2}$ lbs (675g) ripe peach pulp
   liquor from 2 ripe bananas
   3 lbs (1350g) sugar
   2 tsp pectolase
   1 tsp nutrients
   1 vit B tablet
   C.W.E. Formula 67 (Madeira or Tarragona) yeast

Dry:
   1½ lbs (675g) bilberries
   1 lb (450g) ripe peach pulp
   2½ lbs (1125g) sugar
   1 tsp pectolase
   1 tsp nutrients
   1 vit B tablet
   C.W.E. Formula 67 (or Pommard) yeast

Method:
Normal pulp fermentation, with an acid rectification, especially for the dry.

Blackberry and Pineapple

Sweet:
   2½ lbs (1125g) blackberries
   1 ripe pineapple (large)
   1 lb (450g) chopped raisins or sultanas
   2¾ lbs (1250g) sugar
   1 tsp nutrients
   1 vit B tablet
   C.W.E. Formula 67 (or Madeira) yeast

Dry:
   2 lb (900g) blackberries
   1 ripe pineapple (medium)
   2½ lbs (1125g) sugar
   1 tsp nutrients
   1 vit B tablet
   C.W.E. Formula 67 (or Pommard) yeast

Method:
Remove all of the skin from a pineapple which has been allowed to ripen rather more than you would expect for eating. Chop the flesh into 1 inch (2½ cm) cubes, roughly. Mash this as far as possible

with the blackberries. Proceed in the normal way. The dry wine, in particular, will be far too acid unless you adjust.

Cherry and Blackberry

Sweet:
   2 lbs (900g) black cherries (stoned)
   1½ lbs (675g) blackberries
   liquor from 2 ripe bananas
   3 lbs (1350g) sugar
   1 tsp nutrients
   1 vit B tablet
   C.W.E. Formula 67 (or Port) yeast

Dry:
   2 lbs (900g) black cherries (stoned)
   ½ lb (225g) blackberries
   ½ lb (225g) chopped raisins or sultanas
   2½ lbs (1125g) sugar
   1 tsp nutrients
   1 vit B tablet
   C.W.E. Formula 67 (or Bordeaux) yeast

Method:
Normal pulp fermentation. Adjust the acidity.

Dried and Fresh Elderberries
   You can seek the best of both worlds with a mix of the two types of elderberry. The lesser harshness of the dried berries and the fruitier flavour and the better colour of the fresh variety can combine well. The wine will not take as long to mature as a normal elderberry.

Sweet:
   ¾ lb (350g) dried elderberries

1¼ lb (1000g) fresh elderberries
liquor from 2–3 ripe bananas
½ lb (225g) chopped raisins or sultanas
3 lbs (1350g) sugar
1½ tsp citric or citric/tartaric acid
1 tsp nutrients
1 vit B tablet
C.W.E. Formula 67 (or Port) yeast

Dry:
½ lb (225g) dried elderberries
1 lb (450g) fresh elderberries
liquor from 1 ripe banana
2½ lbs (1125g) sugar
1 tsp citric or citric/tartaric acid
1 tsp nutrients
1 vit B tablet
C.W.E. Formula 67 (or Pommard) yeast

Method:
Mash the fresh elderberries in layers, add the dried and pour hot
liquors over the fruit. Cool and proceed as normal.

Elderberry and Apple

Sweet:
2 lbs (900g) elderberries
pulp (liquidised) or extracted juice from 4 lbs (1800g) apples
½ lb (225g) chopped sultanas
2¾ lbs (1250g) sugar
1 tsp nutrients
1 vit B tablet
C.W.E. Formula 67 (or General Purpose) yeast

Dry:
1½ lbs (675g) elderberries

pulp (liquidised) or extracted juice from 3 lbs (1350g) apples
2½ lbs (1125g) sugar
1 tsp nutrients
1 vit B tablet
C.W.E. Formula 67 (or General Purpose) yeast

Method:
As normal. The acidity will be variable and particular attention is required for the dry, which will also take a fair time to mature.

Elderberry and Grapefruit

Sweet:
2½ lb (1125g) elderberries
juice of 6 ripe grapefruit
3 lbs (1350g) sugar
1 tsp nutrients
1 vit B tablet
C.W.E. Formula 67 (or General Purpose) yeast

Method:
Extract the juice from the grapefruit with a lemon squeezer and reject all flesh and pips. Do not add any zest when using citrus fruit in mixed recipes. Otherwise proceed as for a normal pulp fermentation.

Elderberry and Parsnip
This is a combination of the two supposedly most traditional of ingredients, one of which is sound and the other slightly suspect.

Sweet:
2½ lbs (1125g) elderberries
liquor from 4 lbs (1800g) parsnips
3 lbs (1350g) sugar
2 tsp citric or citric/tartaric acid

84

1 tsp pectolase
1 tsp nutrients
1 vit B tablet
C.W.E. Formula 67 (or General Purpose) yeast

Method:
Peel the parsnips, rather than scrub them, and chop into small
chunks. Boil for 15 minutes (taking care that they do not break
up in the water) and discard the pulp. You can pour the hot liquor
over the elderberries after you have mashed them in the usual way.

Gooseberry and Green Elderberry

Sweet:
    $2\frac{1}{2}$ lbs (1125g) gooseberries (mostly ripe, but a few green)
    1 lb (450g) green elderberries
    3 lbs (1350g) sugar
    $\frac{1}{4}$ tsp grape tannin
    1 tsp pectolase
    1 tsp nutrients
    1 vit B tablet
    C.W.E. Formula 67 (or General Purpose) yeast

Dry:
    2 lbs (900g) green gooseberries
    $\frac{3}{4}$ lb (325–350g) green elderberries
    $\frac{1}{2}$ lb (225g) chopped sultanas
    $2\frac{1}{2}$ lbs (1125g) sugar
    $\frac{1}{4}$ tsp grape tannin
    1 tsp pectolase
    1 tsp nutrients
    1 vit B tablet
    C.W.E. Formula 67 (or General Purpose) yeast

Method:
The green gooseberries will need chopping or mincing. Otherwise,
this is a normal pulp method with an acid adjustment.

Gooseberry and Tangerine

Sweet:
  2 lbs (900g) ripe gooseberries
  juice from 3 lbs (1350g) of tangerines (or satsumas)
  liquor from 2–3 ripe bananas
  $\frac{1}{2}$ lb (225g) chopped sultanas
  3 lbs (1350g) sugar
  $\frac{1}{4}$ tsp grape tannin
  1 tsp nutrients
  1 vit B tablet
  C.W.E. Formula 67 (or Riesling) yeast

Dry:
  $1\frac{1}{2}$ lbs (675g) green gooseberries
  juice from 2 lbs (900g) tangerines (or satsumas)
  $\frac{1}{2}$ lb (225g) chopped sultanas
  $2\frac{1}{2}$ lbs (1125g) sugar
  $\frac{1}{4}$ tsp grape tannin
  1 tsp nutrients
  1 vit B tablet
  C.W.E. Formula 67 (or Chablis) yeast

Method:
Avoid any peel, pith or pips from the tangerines – use only the juice. The gooseberries will need chopping or mincing, especially those for the dry wine (which is particularly light and delicate). You will almost certainly have to reduce the acidity.

Plum and Gooseberry

Sweet:
  2 lbs (900g) ripe gooseberries
  $1\frac{1}{2}$ lbs (675g) Victoria plums
  liquor from 1 ripe banana
  $\frac{1}{2}$ lb (225g) chopped sultanas

$2\frac{3}{4}$ lbs (1250g) sugar
1 tsp pectolase
$\frac{1}{4}$ tsp grape tannin
1 tsp nutrients
1 vit B tablet
C.W.E. Formula 67 (or General Purpose) yeast

Method:
Split and stone the plums, cut the gooseberries and mash for a normal method. An acid test will be necessary.

Rosehip and Apple
Make certain that your rosehips are soft and sticky for this wine, rather than hard in the shell. The mix of apples can be mainly dessert with just half a pound or so of cookers (e.g. Bramleys). At all costs avoid using any crab apples in this recipe.

Sweet:
$2\frac{1}{2}$ lbs (1125g) rosehips
pulp (liquidised) or extracted juice from $3–3\frac{1}{2}$ lbs (1350–1500g) apples
$\frac{1}{2}$ lb (225g) chopped sultanas
3 lbs (1350g) sugar
$\frac{1}{4}$ tsp grape tannin
1 tsp pectolase
1 tsp nutrients
1 vit B tablet
C.W.E. Formula 67 (or Sauternes) yeast

Dry:
2 lbs (900g) rosehips
pulp (liquidised) or extracted juice from $2–2\frac{1}{2}$ lbs (900–1125g) apples
$2\frac{1}{2}$ lbs (1125g) sugar
$\frac{1}{4}$ tsp grape tannin
1 tsp pectolase

1 tsp nutrients
1 vit B tablet
C.W.E. Formula 67 (or Chablis) yeast

Method:
The rosehips will have to be crushed or minced. Otherwise proceed in the normal way.

Finally, for now, an example of the sort of potential which is available to us in mixing ingredients:

Combination Red Wine

Sweet:

$1\frac{3}{4}$ lbs (750g) each of any 2 of –

loganberries
bilberries
dewberries
blackberries

liquor from 3 ripe bananas
3 lbs (1350g) sugar
1 tsp pectolase
1 tsp nutrients
1 vit B tablet
C.W.E. Formula 67 (or Port) yeast

Dry:

$1\frac{1}{4}$ lbs (550g) each of any 2 of –

loganberries
bilberries
dewberries
blackberries

liquor from 1 ripe banana
$2\frac{1}{2}$ lbs (1125g) sugar
1 tsp pectolase
1 tsp nutrients
1 vit B tablet
C.W.E. Formula 67 (or Pommard) yeast

Method:
Normal pulp fermentation with an acid check.

CHAPTER 12

Wines to Avoid

It can be a painful, protracted business for the new winemaker who has a natural instinct to try every new ingredient for which he can find a recipe. Even those who have been gathering experience for years cannot have tried everything. The second stage of a winemaker's hobby is to abandon this practice and to become selective. A little guidance might hopefully short-cut this path to discerning experience.

Any dismissal of types of wine or specific recipes must be subjective. What I find repugnant another may enjoy. Nevertheless, a general appreciation of the balance necessary to produce a good wine can call into question whole classes of recipe – the chances of success from many old-fashioned concepts are remote. Books are still published which strive to include every historical recipe possible. We have moved forward since grandmother's day.

FLOWER WINES

It is about time that the fallacy of making flower wines was exposed. Perfume and pollen are not a sound basis for wine.

Expert winemakers will tell you that they add a few ounces of petals (dried or fresh) to their exhibition wines in the hope of catching the judge's nose. It is true that several of our better ingredients lack bouquet. This approach is of course to use flowers as an adjunct not a principal ingredient.

However, you will still find recipes which advocate several pints of flower heads, three pounds of sugar and a yeast. What sort of wine can this produce? There is no body, no vinosity and no character. The likely results are either a stuck fermentation or a low alcohol, low flavour toilet-water. If you insist upon making flower wines, base them upon 1 lb (450g) of chopped sultanas, the

Elderflower   *E. L. Tombs*

liquor from 2 ripe bananas, 2 teaspoons of citric or citric/tartaric acid and $\frac{1}{4}$ teaspoon of grape tannin. Even if you do this, you may well end up with a disappointment.

The best flower wines are made from rose petals (normally red, to give a rosé) and elderflower. The latter is not to everyone's taste, but it is traditional. Be careful how much elderflower you use – the end-product can produce a taste which might well appeal only to cats!

Dandelion and cowslip are recommended by some authorities, but recipes should be approached with great caution. Under no circumstances bother with lilac, lavender, golden rod, carnation or marigold.

In fact, unless you are a proven flower wine lover, do not waste your time on such recipes at all.

ROOT VEGETABLES

Parsnip and beetroot are the only wines in this category worth making and I have considerable reservations about them. Such a statement is obviously treading on hallowed ground, but it must be made. Every time someone tells you that a carrot or potato wine tastes like whisky, take a deep breath. Wines should be made from fruit, not vegetables. Spirits are made by professionals who use a still, not a fermentation jar.

However much one tries to contrive a recipe by fabricating body (bananas), a fruit base (e.g. sultanas), bite (grape tannin) and acid, one can only produce a wine within the limitations of the principal ingredient. Vegetable wines tend to be raw and to require years of maturing to produce anything palatable. Even beetroot, which I accept is an old favourite, can have a very earthy taste in its youth and its red colouring seems very unreliable in storage. Incidentally, avoid any recipe which combines beetroot with ginger – it tastes like toothpaste.

Parsnip wine can be acceptable, but it is not always so. It is the natural sweetness in the roots which seems to make it different. Experiment with parsnip recipes if you wish, but I consider that they are best used (with caution) in mixes with more reliable ingredients such as elderberrries.

Turnips, sugar beet and swedes should be avoided at all costs.

In fact, do not make more than the odd, rare incursion into root wines and then do not be too optimistic.

GRAIN WINES

Some writers advocate making plenty of stock wines from grain. Wheat, barley, oats, maize and rice are commonly recommended as a source of winter wines to keep the cellar full. In truth, it takes little knowledge to realise that the extracted starch from grain is hardly the best source of a smooth, attractive flavour.

Many recipes tend to combine the grain with more acceptable ingredients, to be fair. Modern versions of rice and raisin and wheat and orange produce reasonable wines, but they should never be made at the expense of pure fruit wines. If you want to try grain as a substitute for bananas and sultanas as a means of providing body, then do so. For most palates, however, the results are likely to be on the harsh side.

In a similar way to carrots, wheat will produce a wine which catches the back of the throat. To some this is enough to liken it to whisky. To others it is sufficient to suggest alternative uses for the demijohn.

HERB WINES

To put it bluntly, herb or spice wines are poor at their best. Only ginger, which has its own special characteristics, stands out as the exception.

Parsley, lemon-balm and many others have been "brewed" over the years. Do not waste your time on them.

GIMMICK RECIPES

There is no end to the list of strange wines which people make. A few are given below:

> christmas cake
> coffee
> grass cuttings
> lettuce
> marrow rum
> nettle
> oak leaf
> pea pod
> tea
> tomato

I hope that you have grinned at this list. Strangely they are all still produced by intrepid winemakers. Leave them to their weird adventures.

CERTAIN HEDGEROW FRUITS

The hedgerow is our main source of cheap, quality wines, but there are just a few of the plentiful fruits which should be avoided. Haws (the fruit of the hawthorn) are very tempting. They are abundant and mentioned in the same breath as "hips" by the countryman. Their distinctive taste, however, is not a pleasant one. Crab apples are too much of a gamble if used on their own. The level of astringency is such that you are likely to end up with a very bitter wine. Personally, I would not recommend quinces either. They are best used for jams.

Strawberries are a peculiar fruit from a winemaker's point of view. We delight in their special flavour in sweets and lavish cream on them, yet if you try to make a wine there is invariably something wrong. If you have a glut, make a gallon (2–2½ lbs (900–1125g) plus a few ripe bananas) and see what you think. You will need plenty of sugar in your recipe (3¼ lbs–1450g) because the flavour can be overpowering and you need an excess of sugar to cloak this. I have even made a mixed raspberry and strawberry (in the proportion of 2 lbs (900g) raspberies to ½ lb (225g) strawberries) only to find that the strawberry flavour totally dominated that of the much larger amount of raspberries. If you do try them, you will probably come to the same conclusion as I – the strong, individualistic tang of strawberries is just not suited to wines. Certainly, never try to concoct a dry wine from them.

CERTAIN DRIED FRUITS

Most fruits which are dried for the winemaker are obviously acceptable, or there would be insufficient market for them. However, dried rowanberries and dried juniper berries should be left on the shelf.

Many wines are made from more common domestic dried fruits. I am thinking of figs, prunes and dates. In fact, excellent exhibition wines are made from them and recipes for "sherries" and "ports" are quite common. You need to be something of an expert in this branch of the hobby to achieve success. Too often wines from these sources are unpleasant. You will need trial and error to gain the necessary expertise and, unless you already have this, it is probably best to treat such recipes with suspicion and look for an alternative.

It does not take a great deal of common sense to spot a bad recipe. If the adjustment between flavour, body and "vinosity" looks wrong, be careful. Several unbalanced recipes should give you reason to question the book which you are reading. If you are searching for a new wine, choose flavours which are known to you. Otherwise, take your recipe from a reputable text book or periodical. Never invest your time or money in a batch of over one gallon if you have any reservations at all about the wine you are making.

CHAPTER 13

Introducing Modern Ingredients

The tendency to convenience wines has brought a new class of ingredients into prominence. Winemakers are becoming lazy and far too happily settle for second best. Tinned fruit and fruit juice concentrates are far more common in the fermentation jar than they should be.

However, if we examine some of these products we can find potential for our country wines, if not for definite improvement, then for variation. By introducing modern convenience ingredients we can extend our season and, more importantly, the range of mixes available to us when designing our must.

Tinned Fruit

A common simple recipe, which you will find in many text books published in recent years, is:

2 lbs (900g) tinned fruit
½ lb (225g) chopped sultanas
2 lbs (900g) sugar
2 tsp pectolase
½ tsp tannin
2 tsp acid (unless an acid fruit is being used)
1 tsp nutrients
1 vit B tablet
General Purpose yeast

The method advocated is normally to liquidise or mash the fruit, strain, ferment to dryness as quickly as possible and add saccharine to taste. Some recipes even drop the fruit content to a 1 lb (450g) can – this level is wholly inadequate.

Such methods provide you with a quick "plonk", which to my mind is characterless. There are a lot of tinned fruits which, when used in these minimal quantities, will give you a feeble wine. With the exception of highly flavoured fruits (such as blackcurrants and raspberries) there is an argument for using up to 4 lbs (1800g) of fruit per gallon. At this point, of course, the economy factor in making "quickie" wines begins to be lost.

Tinned fruit does not taste the same as a fresh fruit salad. The wines made from it definitely lack something and they are not recommended as a substitute for good country wines. If you are totally at a loss in February as to how to fill your demijohn, then by all means try one of these wines (preferably with a minimum of 3–3½ lbs (1350–1600g) of tinned fruit), but do not set out with a great deal of optimism.

More significant is the potential of using tinned fruit within a sound recipe rather than on its own. If you find yourself with just a moderately sized bag of blackberries left in the freezer, you could try something along these lines:

Blackberry and Tinned Loganberry

Dry:
1½ lbs (675g) blackberries
2 × 1 lb (2 × 450g) tins of loganberries
1½ lbs (675g) sugar
1 tsp pectolase
1 tsp nutrients
1 vit B tablet
C.W.E. Formula 67 (or General Purpose) yeast

Sweet:
You should be able to concoct a suitable recipe for a sweet wine from the above, by now. Slightly more fruit will be necessary, and a further ½ lb (225g) of sugar. A sweet wine needs increased body, so bananas or chopped sultanas will improve the balance. A suitable adjustment would be:

2 lbs (900g) blackberries
3 × 1 lb (3 × 450g) tins of loganberries
liquor from 2 ripe bananas (or ½ lb (225g) of chopped sultanas)
1¼ lbs (550g) sugar
1 tsp pectolase
1 tsp nutrients
1 vit B tablet
C.W.E. Formula 67 (or General Purpose) yeast

We can try a few more recipes along the same lines. The only guess is the correct sugar content, unless you monitor your Original Gravity. If we start with a conservative amount of sugar the wine can always be fed with more in its later life.

Elderberry and Tinned Cherry

Sweet:
1½ lbs (675g) elderberries

Some quite exotic fruits can now be bought in tins and are worth experiments.

3 × 1 lb (3 × 450g) tins of black cherrries
liquor from 3 ripe bananas
1$\frac{3}{4}$ lbs (800g) sugar
1 tsp pectolase
1 tsp nutrients
1 vit B tablet
C.W.E. Formula 67 (or Port) yeast

Dry:
    1$\frac{1}{4}$ lbs (550g) elderberries
    2 × 1 lb (2 × 450g) tins of black cherries
    1$\frac{1}{2}$ lbs (675g) sugar
    1 tsp pectolase
    1 tsp nutrients
    1 vit B tablet
    C.W.E. Formula 67 (or Pommard) yeast

Gooseberry and Tinned Apple

Sweet:
    2 lbs (900g) ripe gooseberries
    3 lb (1350g) tin of apple pulp
    liquor from 2 ripe bananas
    1$\frac{3}{4}$ lbs (800g) sugar
    1 tsp pectolase
    $\frac{1}{4}$ tsp grape tannin
    1 tsp nutrients
    1 vit B tablet
    C.W.E. Formula 67 (or Riesling) yeast

Dry:
    1$\frac{1}{2}$ lbs (675g) green gooseberries
    2 lbs (900g) tin of apple pulp
    1$\frac{1}{2}$ lbs (675g) sugar
    1 tsp pectolase
    $\frac{1}{4}$ tsp grape tannin

1 tsp nutrients
1 vit B tablet
C.W.E. Formula 67 (or Chablis) yeast

Gooseberry and Tinned Pear

Sweet:
   2 lbs (900g) ripe gooseberries
   2 × 1 lb (2 × 450g) tins of pears
   liquor from 3 ripe bananas
   $1\frac{3}{4}$ lbs (800g) sugar
   1 tsp pectolase
   $\frac{1}{4}$ tsp grape tannin
   1 tsp nutrients
   1 vit B tablet
   C.W.E. Formula 67 (or Riesling) yeast

Dry:
   2 lbs (900g) green gooseberries
   1 tin (1 lb – 450g) of pears
   $\frac{1}{2}$ lb (225g) chopped sultanas
   $1\frac{1}{2}$ lbs (675g) sugar
   1 tsp pectolase
   $\frac{1}{4}$ tsp grape tannin
   1 tsp nutrients
   1 vit B tablet
   C.W.E. Formula 67 (or Chablis) yeast

Loganberry and Tinned Raspberry

Sweet:
   $2\frac{1}{2}$ lbs (1125g) loganberries
   1 tin (450g – 1 lb) of raspberries
   liquor from 3 ripe bananas
   $2\frac{1}{4}$ lbs (1000g) sugar
   1 tsp pectolase

1 tsp nutrients
1 vit B tablet
C.W.E. Formula 67 (or any sweet red wine culture) yeast

Dry:
2 lbs (900g) loganberries
1 tin (1 lb – 450g) of raspberries
liquor from 1 ripe banana
2 lbs (900g) sugar
1 tsp pectolase
1 vit B tablet
1 tsp nutrients
C.W.E. Formula 67 (or any dry red wine culture) yeast

Method:
The basic approach need not vary from our normal pulp fermentation, except that the inclusion of green gooseberries will involve chopping or mincing them. It is, however, often recommended that tinned fruit be liquidised before it is introduced into the must. This practice does encourage maximum extraction of flavour and can only be of help.

You will need to add more sugar to these wines, as I have erred on the cautious side. Do this by adding in 4 oz (110g) batches (as cooled syrup) when the gravity drops to 1.000. Obviously, be careful in doing this that you do not leave unwanted residual sugar in a dry wine.

The acidity of tinned fruit varies, like the sugar content, from brand to brand and a check at some stage is certainly advisable.

From these example recipes you will see that the potential for incorporating convenience ingredients into our wines is considerable, providing that we use them as a secondary fruit rather than as a sole base for a wine. There are limitless combinations and thus plenty of scope for experiment. These possibilities are discussed in more detail in the following chapter.

Pure Fruit Juices

Pure apple, orange, lime, grapefruit, lemon, blackcurrant and many other juices are available in supermarkets etc. and are becoming more common in use for quick, easy wines. Again, I have reservations about them as sole ingredients. The end-products are rather thin and unconvincing.

Use only unsweetened pure juices (in cartons or cans) and make sure that they do not contain a preservative – this will inhibit your yeast if it is present.

If you want to try one of these "soft-option" wines, you should be now be able to construct your own recipe along these lines:

Sweet:

3 pints approx. (2 litres) unsweetened fruit juice
$\frac{1}{2}$ lb (225g) chopped sultanas
liquor from 2 ripe bananas (optional)
3 lbs (1350g) sugar
1 tsp pectolase
$\frac{1}{4}$ tsp grape tannin
1 tsp nutrients
1 vit B tablet
C.W.E. Formula 67 (or General Purpose) yeast

If you fancy something more enterprising and likely to give you a wine of greater character, you must start with a decent fruit base. For a winter fermentation, the following will give you a pleasant sweet red:

$\frac{3}{4}$ lb (350g) dried elderberries
$1\frac{1}{2}$ pints (approx. 1 litre) of unsweetened orange juice
liquor from 2 ripe bananas
3 lbs (1350g) sugar
1 tsp pectolase
1 tsp nutrients
1 vit B tablet
C.W.E. Formula 67 (or General Purpose) yeast

Here are a few more ideas for incorporating pure fruit juices into wines made with a sound base ingredient:

Bilberry and Blackcurrant Juice

Sweet:
2 lbs (900g) fresh bilberries
1 pint (0.6 litre) Ribena, C-Vit or similar
liquor from 2 ripe bananas
$\frac{1}{2}$ lb (225g) chopped sultanas
2 lbs (900g) sugar
1 tsp nutrients
1 vit B tablet
C.W.E. Formula 67 (or General Purpose) yeast

Dry:
$\frac{3}{4}$ lb (350g) dried bilberries
$\frac{3}{4}$ pint ($\frac{1}{2}$ litre) Ribena, C-Vit or similar
$\frac{1}{2}$ lb (225g) chopped sultanas
2 lbs (900g) sugar
1 tsp nutrients
1 vit B tablet
C.W.E. Formula 67 (or General Purpose) yeast

Grape and Lemon Juice

Sweet:
6–8 lbs (2700–3600g) grapes
1 litre of pure lemon juice
liquor from 2 ripe bananas
$1\frac{1}{2}$ lbs (675g) sugar
1 tsp pectolase
1 tsp nutrients
1 vit B tablet
C.W.E. Formula 67 (or Sauternes) yeast

Dry:
5–6 lbs (2250–2700g) grapes

1 pint (0.6 litre) of pure lemon juice
liquor from 1 ripe banana
1¼ lbs (1000g) sugar
1 tsp pectolase
1 tsp nutrients
1 vit B tablet
C.W.E. Formula 67 (or Chablis) yeast

A Touch of the Caribbean

Sweet:
    1 medium pineapple (very ripe)
    juice of 3 grapefruits
    1 litre of tropical fruit juice (passion fruit etc.)
    liquor from 3 ripe bananas
    ½ lb (225g) chopped sultanas
    2½ lbs (1125g) sugar
    ¼ tsp grape tannin
    2 tsp pectolase
    1 tsp nutrients
    1 vit B tablet
    C.W.E. Formula 67 (or General Purpose) yeast

Methods:
The basic method for these mixed wines is a normal pulp fermentation for 7 days or so before straining. If using a recipe which
incorporates fresh grapes, be careful to buy the smaller varieties
rather than the large dessert types. Wash grapes well and crush
them in a bucket. Avoid the pips and skin by straining – you can
go directly into the demijohn with the two recipes above.

Specialist Concentrates
    Elderberry concentrate, rosehip puree, highly concentrated apple
and various other types of tinned specialist products are available
to the winemaker. Full instructions for making the wines are given
with these ingredients. More interesting wines, however, can be
made by using half of the recommended quantity and incorporating
this with fresh fruit along the lines of the examples given above.

CHAPTER 14

Experimenting Further: Creating your own Recipes

The culmination of the second stage of a winemaker's progress is to arrive at a point where he can create his own recipes with confidence. Many are hesitant to take this step, although they have probably already adjusted existing recipes without realising it.

At the end of Chapter 11 we looked at a combination wine (any two of four similar berries) and in our brief examination of modern, convenience ingredients we saw the possibilities of bringing in tinned or fresh fruit products as secondary fruits. The ability to judge the flavour combinations and balance of a must is not really a difficult one.

Firstly we must eliminate or qualify those of our First and Second Division fruits which we should omit or only incorporate with caution:

Birch Sap – it is total waste to hide the delicacy of this subtle specialist wine by losing it in a combination recipe. Use your birch sap for the recommended recipe.

Blackcurrants – due to the strong flavour (and high acidity) blackcurrants are best used in small batches only, when mixing. $\frac{1}{2}-\frac{3}{4}$ lb (225–350g) should be treated as a maximum, except in mixes with redcurrants, where it is traditional to use rather more.

Ginger – avoid the temptation to incorporate ginger, as it can be overpowering.

Pomegranate – again it is the distinctive flavour which suggests that these strange fruit should be kept to themselves.

Raspberries – I always incorporate ½ lb (225g) or so of raspberries in a port-style wine because they give that little tang of fruitiness. However, much more than this amount to the gallon is likely to prove excessively dominant.

Rhubarb – often recommended for combining with red fruits, rhubarb is in fact not a particularly good mixer. Try it if you wish but be sure to employ the special method of extraction referred to in the individual recipe.

Other Fruits

Strawberries – as has already been discussed, if you are tempted to use strawberries in combination with other fruit, you will be disappointed. If you must use them, substitute for raspberry in the individual recipe.

Beetroot – only parsnips, of the root vegetables, are a reasonable mixer. Certainly beetroot, with its unusual characteristics, is best kept to itself.

Having removed a few items from our potential combinations, we can find others to add in their place:

Garden Fruits

Blueberries – various types of Scottish or American blueberries are available to the gardener. Substitute them for bilberries if you wish to use them on their own. They make excellent wines.

Huckleberries – these are an annual which thus have the advantage of growing from seed to ripeness in a single season. The plant itself looks like one of the nightshades, so be a little careful. The black, spherical berries are bitter to the taste but can be used for sweet wine. About 2 lbs (900g) to the gallon is sufficient. In a combination wine use no more than ½ lb (225g) of huckleberries.

Kiwi Fruit – the mail order garden firms advertise kiwi fruit nowadays. At around 25p per fruit in the shops, the ability to make a gallon from $2\frac{1}{2}$–3 lbs (1125–1350g) is beyond the normal pocket. Growing your own (you need plants of both sexes) will take a few years but at least it might enable you to try them in a fermentation. You might find that you need a fair amount of "banana body" but the results should be interesting.

Mulberries – use only in small amounts in mixes because of their distinctive flavour.

Raspberry/Blackberry crosses – apart from the loganberry there are several other lesser-known varieties which you can grow, such as the Marionberry. These can be substituted for loganberries in the individual recipes or used successfully in your own combined recipes.

Tayberries – they are relatively expensive plants to buy, but an excellent fruit. Tayberries can be used to replace either blackberries or loganberries in the recipes given. They mix well if you are creating a red wine.

Dried Fruit
Dried elderberries and bilberries have already been discussed, and they both make an excellent base for a mixed ingredient wine. In addition, you can purchase the following dried fruits from specialist shops:

> apricots
> peaches
> rosehip shells
> sloes

All of these are useful to the winemaker. The apricots and peaches should be soaked for 24 hours before use and pectolase should be present during this process. Otherwise you can boil them to extract the flavour and add pectolase to the extraction when it has cooled.

Do not use two dried ingredients in the same recipe (with the exception of dried grapes – i.e. raisins or sultanas). A fruit from our list of favourites, a tinned fruit or a fresh juice should be your objective in looking for a complementary fruit for dried ingredients. Also, bear in mind that dried fruits tend to be deficient in body and (usually) in acid.

The Modern Philosophy

The aims of the selective winemaker who has progressed beyond the first few steps of the hobby can be summarised as follows:

1. To produce a main stream of the proven, traditional wines.
2. To reject those traditional ingredients which give a likelihood of inferior wines, regardless of some conventional recipes.
3. Without attempting a facsimile of the grape, to have regard to the proper constituents of a balanced must.
4. To incorporate, with care, fruits available in tinned form or as pulps or juices, but to avoid using them alone except for very basic wines.
5. To use the experience of sound recipes and an appreciation of the requirements of a balanced must to create new recipes from available fruits.

The Balanced Must

Fruit Content

There are exceptions, which should be evident from the individual recipes given earlier for strongly flavoured wines, but generally we need:

Sweet 3–3½ lbs (1350g–1500g) fruit (or equivalent)

Dry 2½–2¾ lbs (1125g–1250g) fruit (or equivalent)

Equivalents –
  1 lb (450g) dried fruit = 2½ lbs (1125g) fresh
  1 lb (450g) tinned fruit = ¾ lb (350g) fresh
  1 litre fruit juice = 1 lb (450g) fresh
  (approx.)

106

Thus we can think in terms of formulating a gallon of wine from any of the following:

$\frac{1}{2}$ lb (225g) dried fruit with 2 lbs (900g) fresh fruit
$1\frac{1}{2}$ lbs (550g) fresh fruit with 2 lbs (900g) tinned fruit
$\frac{3}{4}$ lb (350g) dried fruit with 1 litre of fresh juice and so on.

Dry wines can be formulated from the above equivalents simply by a reduction of $\frac{1}{2}$–$\frac{3}{4}$ lb (225–300g) in weight (in fresh fruit terms).

Sugar Content
We need 3 lbs (1350g) total sugar for a sweet wine and $2\frac{1}{2}$ lbs (1250g) for a dry. Virtually all fruits contain their own sugar and your prepared must will have an initial content from the fruit alone. Normally this natural sugar plus the 3 lbs/$2\frac{1}{2}$ lbs addition will happily be accommodated by a good yeast and problems are unlikely to arise.

However, we are including tinned fruits in our mixes and I would suggest a cautious approach to these. Deduct $\frac{1}{2}$ lb (225g) per 1 lb (450g) tin of fruit as a starting point. You can always feed the wine with additional 4 oz (110g) amounts when it ferments down to dryness. Better safe than sorry – and there is nothing more sorry than an oversweet wine.

If you are using raisins or sultanas deduct half their weight as sugar. Grape concentrate should be deducted at the rate of $\frac{3}{4}$ lb per pint (say 450g per litre), again erring on the careful side.

Body
Have a look at your fruit formula and decide whether you need additional body. For sweet wines you can add the liquor from 1–4 bananas, for dry wines settle for 1 or 2. If you are using grape concentrate in any quantity, halve the amount of bananas.

Vinosity
I suppose that vinosity means grape-like qualities. As such, it does not stand much examination in relation to my suggested philosophy for the winemaker. We are taking our yardstick of balance within the must from the grape, but we are not attempting an artificial, direct copy.

However, the grape qualities of raisins or sultanas, which we often use for body and "boost", are a bonus. Obviously if we incorporate grape concentrate then we are bringing this factor into prominence. But "vinosity" need not be an objective in itself.

Acidity

Acidity is our greatest problem. Firstly, our fruits contain predominantly either citric or malic acid whereas the grape has tartaric acid. Secondly, the grape has its own natural balance of acidity which is eminently suitable for wine production. Our fruits almost invariably require some sort of adjustment.

Judgement on this point is needed when the recipe is structured. Acid should be added (normally in the quantity of one or two teaspoons of acid crystals) to ingredients lacking in the element. This applies to such low-acid fruits as dried fruits, ripe gooseberries and elderberries, whereas, of course, no acid addition should be made to citrus fruits, rhubarb, blackberries or the like. About the most ideally balanced fruits which we have available to us are bilberries, dewberries and well-ripened peach.

The question of acid adjustment merits a chapter of its own, and is dealt with later.

Tannin

The presence of tannin is necessary for three reasons. Firstly, it adds a touch of astringency which gives a wine bite. Secondly, it improves the keeping qualities of wines – this is one explanation for the fact that red wines (with their natural tannin content) tend to keep and mature better than white ones. Thirdly, tannin aids the natural clearing process and without it there is a good chance of a hazy end-product.

Damsons, elderberries and sloes have more than enough tannin – it is a problem rather than a bonus. Some authorities recommend fining with a tablespoon or two of beaten egg white per gallon before bottling to reduce this astringency.

Grape tannin powder or liquid can be purchased quite easily. It is produced from the dried skin and pips of grapes and is perfect for the job. As a rule of thumb add $\frac{1}{4}$ teaspoon to all musts which will have a deficiency. You can always add more before you bottle if the wine is bland.

Bouquet

My recipes in this book pay little regard to bouquet, because I feel that an unnatural bouquet in a wine is worse than a low bouquet. For instance, a dry blackberry has a smell all of its own and the benefits of adding dried or fresh flower petals are debatable.

I leave the choice to you. Heavy, fruity wines will be better suited to this sort of treatment than light, subtle ones.

There is a large variety of dried flowers on the market. Avoid the stranger types – half an ounce of dried elderflowers or dried rose-petals will be the safest bet.

Pectin Control

A high level of pectin will give you a stubbornly cloudy wine which will cause you great frustration. Those fruits which have a high pectin content include apricots, damsons, peaches and plums and the addition of 2–3 teaspoons of pectolase (which is an enzyme and operates as a catalyst in the process of breaking down the fruit) is essential. Add this only when your must has cooled. As well as aiding clarification the enzyme will also assist to some extent in the disintegration of the fruit during the pulp fermentation and so help with extraction of flavour.

Getting Started

If we start with an ancillary package of

liquor of 2 ripe bananas
3 lbs (1350g) sugar (2½ lbs – 1125g for a dry wine)
2 tsp pectolase
¼ tsp grape tannin
1 tsp citric or citric/tartaric acid
1 tsp nutrients
1 vit B tablet
C.W.E. Formula 67 (or quality yeast culture of your choice)

then all we need is to decide upon our fruits and adjust the package as necessary.

There is no point in giving an extended list of possibilities – the enjoyment of concocting recipes should be yours – but a few examples will give you the idea:

1. **2 lbs (900g) elderberries, 1 pint (0.6 litre) grapefruit juice**
Adjustment – omit tannin, omit acid

2. **2 lbs (900g) blackberries, ½ pint (0.3 litre) blackcurrant cordial (Ribena etc.), ½ pint (0.3 litre) orange juice**
Adjustments – omit acid, omit tannin, reduce sugar by 4 oz (100g) to take account of sugar content of the cordial

3. **2 × 1 lb (900g total) tins peach halves, 1½ lbs (675g) fresh gooseberries**
Adjustments – omit acid if gooseberries are green (unripe), double the pectolase, reduce sugar to take account of the syrup in the tinned fruit to 1¾ lbs (800g) for sweet or 1¼ lbs (500g) for dry

4. **½ lb (225g) dried bilberries, 2 × 1 lb (900g total) tins of apricots**
Adjustments – omit tannin, double the pectolase, reduce the sugar as in 3 above.

5. **1 lb (450g) elderberries, ½ lb (225g) dried sloes, 1 pint (0.6 litre) pure orange juice**
Adjustments – omit acid, omit tannin.

Now have a go yourself.

CHAPTER 15

Acidity Levels

The problem of attaining reasonable acidity has always concerned winemakers. Whether they realised it or not they traditionally diluted their fruit juices down to an acceptable level of acidity, in effect by watering down. When they were faced with a fruit which was in itself low in acidity they added lemon or orange juice. These methods were obviously hit or miss. One batch of peach pulp will be more acid than another. In a hot, dry year blackberries will have a higher acidity than they will in a dull, wet year.

Because of this haphazard attention to acidity in traditional recipes, most winemakers pay scant regard to the problem. They add acid if the recipe says so, but otherwise leave things to chance. In progressing to a second stage of winemaking we must accept that correct acidity levels are essential and eliminate the element of chance as far as possible. The common reluctance to get involved in what seems at first sight a scientific analysis is understandable. In fact, the basic concept is simple.

Acid levels are measured as parts per thousand (p.p.t.) of the volume. The actual yardstick used is that of sulphuric acid, which is hopefully not a type of acid actually present in our wines. It is simply a common denominator by which we can express the acidity of our must.

Obviously, we want the acidity in our wines at the right sort of level from the point of view of taste, but the function of acid goes further than this. Strange flavours can evolve in wines which have insufficient acid – not just a weakness but even an unpleasant bitterness. Maturing (the gradual change in a wine during storage) is largely a product of the interaction between alcohol and acid, so we cannot ignore the equation.

Acidity Levels to be Desired

Dry   3.0–3.5 p.p.t. (light)
Medium   3.5–3.75 p.p.t.
Sweet   3.75–4.5 p.p.t. (normal)
Sweet   4.25–5.0 p.p.t. (full bodied)

Acid Content of Various Ingredients

Item	Main Acid	Common %
Apple	malic	1–3
Banana	citric	$\frac{1}{2}$–1
Bilberry	citric	$\frac{1}{2}$–1
Blackberry	citric	1–2
Blackcurrant	citric	2–3
Cherry	malic	1–1$\frac{3}{4}$
Damson	malic	1$\frac{1}{2}$–2$\frac{1}{2}$
Elderberry	citric	1–2
Gooseberry (green)	malic	1$\frac{1}{2}$–2
Grape	tartaric	$\frac{3}{4}$–2
Loganberry	citric	1$\frac{1}{2}$–2
Peach	malic	1$\frac{1}{2}$–2
Pineapple	citric	1–2
Plum	malic	1–1$\frac{1}{2}$
Raspberry	citric	1$\frac{1}{2}$–2$\frac{1}{2}$
Redcurrant	citric	1$\frac{1}{2}$–3
Rhubarb	malic	2$\frac{1}{2}$–3$\frac{1}{2}$
Root vegetables	–	minimal

From these few examples it becomes obvious not only that fruits vary between each other in their inherent acidity but also that they have a wide range of possible acidity levels in themselves. Acidity will differ from batch to batch. The need for adjustment becomes more and more obvious.

Timing your Check

Most authorities recommend adjusting when you actually prepare the must, prior to introducing the yeast. The problem here is that you want to be testing an exact gallon and not a lesser concentration which will in due course be "watered down" at sieving and racking stages. Obviously if you only have half a gallon (net of fruit pulp) in your fermentation bucket your readings or tastings will be twice as acid as the likely end-product. So be careful – mark your bucket at the gallon level and allow an inch or so above this for the pulp which will be discarded.

Alternatively make your acid check when your wine is ready for bottling. This is the approach advocated in the standard pulp fermentation method in this book. Although it might be frowned upon by the experts, it is easier and arguably more convenient. To my mind, unless you are using a full titration method, just before bottling is the best time to adjust.

Taste

Acid testing by taste is the simplest yet crudest method. It is certainly better than no test at all, but relies upon your taste buds rather than science. If you taste the must before fermentation your judgement might be clouded by the solids and certainly by the sugar level. Better to wait until you are about to bottle.

Sip the wine with a clean palate (a piece of cheese will help). What you are looking for is a *slight* tang of acid. Your recipe notes should give you a fair idea of the likely position.

If your wine tastes bland you will need to add acid. Do this by the gradual addition of citric, tartaric or mixed citric/tartaric acid crystals – half a level teaspoon at a time. Each such dose of $\frac{1}{2}$ tsp will increase the acidity of a gallon of wine by about 0.5 p.p.t.. Swirl to dissolve the crystals fully and taste again. Continue with similar measures until you can detect slight acidity which satisfies you.

If the wine is over-acid, you can reduce by adding "acid reducing liquid", which is usually potassium carbonate solution and can be obtained from most specialist winemaker's stores. The "dose" will be indicated in the instructions. Add on a careful trial basis by the teaspoonful (normally one tsp will reduce the acidity of a gallon by 0.5 p.p.t.), retasting each time after mixing thoroughly.

If you cannot obtain an acid reducing agent of this type, precipitated chalk can be used as a last resort. This is commonly available in multiple stores but should be used only with great care, or you could ruin your wine. Add only small amounts ($\frac{1}{2}$ tsp at a time) and under no circumstances use ½ oz or more. Chalk will leave a deposit in the demijohn and you may even experience a foaming reaction in the wine.

Although the tasting technique is hardly scientific and very subjective, the different acid requirements of dry and sweet wines will to some degree be taken care of automatically by your palate. By this I mean that a sweet wine of 4.5 p.p.t. will taste less acid than a dry wine of 4.5 p.p.t. due to the overlay of fruit and sugar – your adjustments to taste should bring the wine roughly into line with acceptable levels.

Wine Indicator Paper

Much like the litmus paper of the school laboratory, this is merely an acid/alkali indicator by colour. Small rolls of the paper are quite readily available and are best used immediately before bottling. A short strip is torn from the roll and dipped in a sample of the wine. Excess moisture is shaken off and the paper is held for 30 seconds or so. The colour can then be compared with the colour chart of acidities provided with the paper. If adjustment is necessary, it can be made in the way described above. After the

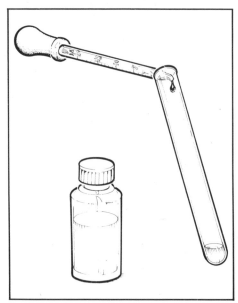

Acidity testing

addition of acid crystals or reducing liquid, as required, a fresh piece of paper is used to check. It is not a difficult task to get your acidity level approximately right with this paper.

Acidity Test Kit

By far the best method of checking and adjusting acidity is by using an acidity testing kit. If you are going to exhibit seriously, you must have one. You should (perhaps after a little practice with trial runs) be able to tell the acidity of your wines to within 0.25 p.p.t. without too much difficulty. These kits are not very expensive and are well worth while.

The system used is by titration. Full instructions are normally included with the kits, but a brief description might serve to remove some of the hesitancy which many winemakers seem to harbour.

A calibrated dropper is used to transfer a precise amount of the wine to a test tube. This is diluted in distilled water (in fact, most tap-waters do not affect results unduly). Some sort of acid indicator solution is then added – it will be supplied with the kit.

The basis of the test is to add sodium hydroxide from the dropper until the solution turns a faint pink. The acidity of your wine will equate to a calculation based upon the amount of the sodium hydroxide necessary to reach this point. The amount of the chemical used is read from the calibrated dropper and this figure is divided by four to give you the acidity of your must or finished wine. Adjustments are then made in the normal way and a check titration taken.

The process might seem difficult in theory, but in practice you will hardly find it demanding.

CHAPTER 16

Stuck Fermentations

A fermentation which sticks and stubbornly refuses to proceed can happen to anyone. It is one of the most common problems a winemaker has to tackle and it can arise when least expected. Our fruits do vary in their suitability for wine and it is thus perhaps not surprising that occasionally we have difficulties in achieving a total fermentation.

The most common point at which the halt can occur is around 1030 SG (sweet wines) or 1020 SG (dry wines). Normally a young yeast is vigorous enough to overcome imbalances, but as it gets older it becomes more sluggish (as the alcohol level increases) and it is at this point that it can become temperamental.

Obviously our aim is to produce wines which will not be likely to "stick". Our balanced musts and calculated sugar and acidity levels will minimise the danger. Ingredients which do not lend themselves to fermentation have been avoided or used only in a suitably adjusted recipe. Nevertheless you cannot be immune from the odd sticking fermentation.

Care should be taken to distinguish between a slow fermentation and a static one. Some wines seem by their nature to be appreciably slower than others (mead is a prime example). If you do not have a source of heating near your demijohn proceedings may pause during winter, when the temperature drops to such a level that the yeast becomes inhibited – in all probability activity will again be apparent when the temperature rises. Bearing this single reservation in mind, you will normally be certain of having a stuck fermentation if the hydrometer reading remains the same over a period of 4–6 weeks. By taking hydrometer readings when you rack and making a note of them you will be able to monitor your fermentations with confidence.

The possible causes of sticking, and their cures, are listed below:

No Yeast Present

This may seem a strange occurrence at first sight, but it is fairly common. The balanced must, which a good winemaker concentrates upon producing, can "drop clear" when it has become only a young wine – well before fermentation is near completion. When you make your regular rackings there is a danger of siphoning the wine off the yeast so that you have prematurely lost your fermenting agent.

Avoidance is not difficult. Allow a wisp or two of the lees (which will include yeast) to be drawn up the siphon tube on every racking until you reach the final one.

Fresh yeast can be introduced, if necessary, but you will first have to build up its alcohol tolerance. Choose a vigorous general purpose (C.W.E. Formula 67 compound is ideal) and make a starter with about ¼ pint (0.2 litre) of water. Place the started yeast under an airlock (a bung and lock will fit the neck of several types of sterilised milk bottles, if you have nothing better) and add a quarter of a pint (0.2 litre) of the wine. Leave this for about a week and then add a further similar amount. When the diluted wine is fermenting steadily, add it to your demijohn.

As an alternative to a yeast compound such as Formula 67, you can try a Condessa Restart Pack, which contains a "highly active alcohol tolerant yeast".

Abnormal Temperatures

Winemakers normally make certain that they keep their fermenting vessels where they will not be subjected to extreme temperatures. A wine yeast will tolerate quite a remarkable range of temperatures – from 40°F to 85°F – but you can kill it if you go beyond these limits. Exposure to frost (the wine will not normally actually freeze, because of the alcohol present) or to very high temperatures (such as by placing it on top of a central heating boiler) can destroy the yeast. If you suspect either of these extremes as the reason for your stuck fermentation, restart with a vigorous yeast as described above.

Lack of Nutrients

If you accidentally omit these from the must, you can have problems from lack of nitrogen. Yeast needs nutrients and trace elements to foster its well-being. Normally one teaspoon of a suitably good quality grade (C.W.E. brand are excellent) together with a vitamin B tablet will provide all that you need to supplement the natural nutrients of the fruit.

Nevertheless, one of the most common cures for a stuck fermentation is the addition of an extra teaspoon of nutrient salts.

Acetification

When a wine becomes vinegar, fermentation will cease. This particular horror is discussed in the following chapter. Smell and taste will confirm that your wine is acetified. There is no cure – throw it away.

Choking with Sugar

It is possible to suffocate the yeast with an excess of sugar. In practice this is a rare occurrence and the normal safeguard recommended by many of adding the required sugar in doses of 1 lb (450g) or $\frac{1}{2}$ lb (225g) can be followed, if you wish to be particularly cautious. Personally, I do not find the need to do this – it can prolong the length of time in the demijohn by creating delays while the wine is awaiting a hydrometer reading to confirm that it has used all of the sugar. A good yeast will cope with a solution of 3 lbs (1350g) of sugar within a gallon of liquid without undue difficulty.

A sacrometer is an easy means of measuring sugar content at any stage of fermentation. Perhaps not a vital tool, but it simplifies checking progress.

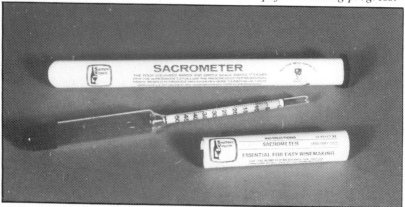

What you must never do is to add sugar in its solid form. Not only will you create an initial foaming reaction, but you will also run the risk of choking the yeast with this blanket of sugar. Always dissolve your sugar addition in hot water, cool and then add.

Yeast Exhausted
When the yeast has reached the limit of its alcohol tolerance, fermentation will cease. This is a finished wine and not a sticking one, of course. If the recipe contained too much sugar, then you can adopt the remedies contained in the following chapter. But if your recipe is checked and it should have been within the capacity of the yeast to progress the fermentation further, then your yeast may be damaged, dead or inadequate for the job. Restarting with C.W.E. Formula 67 yeast compound or a Condessa Restart Pack, as described above, should be tried if you have any doubts at all about your yeast.

Carbon Dioxide in Solution
If the carbon dioxide given off during fermentation is not allowed to escape, it can be absorbed into liquid and inhibit the yeast. This is a rare happening, usually caused by a blocked air-lock. Providing a reliable lock is fitted you can discount this possibility.

Insufficient Air
There must be a certain amount of oxygen absorbed into the wine for the yeast to thrive. Its requirements, in fact, are minimal but if you rack without splashing and fill your demijohn close to the bottom of its neck in the later stages you could have trouble.

In practice experienced winemakers have no problems in keeping oxygen levels adequate. They are normally far more concerned with avoiding oxidisation of the wine due to it absorbing too much air.

If you allow a *little* splashing during racking, or pour your wine back into its original (cleaned) demijohn gently, you will be unlikely to have problems on either score. If you leave a couple of inches (but not four inches or more) as a depth of air gap between the level of wine and the bottom of the neck of the jar during fermentation you can hardly go wrong. Remember also that a regular glance at your air-locks will reveal whether they need topping up with water. Oxidisation is dealt with later.

Lack of Acid or Body

Enough stress has been placed upon the need for a balanced must, and in particular in designing recipes which will approximate to the correct acidity level, for it to be obvious that a failure in these areas can create an unreliable fermentation.

It must be remembered that we are using grape wine yeasts. Whereas we are not attempting to make an identical copy of a Moselle or a Reisling, we do need a grape-style balance of chemicals and body in our must. Thus it is inevitable that we are trying, in broad terms, to reproduce the grape's characteristics. This approach need not be the obsession some would have you believe – if your recipe caters for adequate flavour and bite it will tend to be right for a reliable fermentation.

Many old-fashioned recipes should suggest a stuck fermentation to the reader by their make-up. Flower wines and vegetable wines were often made in a way which could never provide enough body and nutrition for the yeast and very rarely sufficient acid. Avoid dodgy recipes. An example that springs to mind is a blackcurrant wine made solely from a bottle of Ribena (or the like) and sugar – such "thin" musts seem to take an eternity to ferment out and are disappointing in any event when they eventually do.

Bear in mind also that many authors are often optimistic in the times they estimate for fermentation. Probably they are over-conscious of the modern impatience. Three or four months in the demijohn is quite normal for a good country wine. Six months is not remarkable. Be patient and do not diagnose a fermentation as stuck until you have taken several hydrometer readings over a period of time.

Finally, if all else fails with your stubborn wine which has stopped at around SG 1.030, try an old-fashioned remedy. Chop a handful of raisins or sultanas and drop them into the demijohn. The grape, in its dried form, could be your saviour.

CHAPTER 17

Disorders – Avoidance and Cures

Most authors list the horrors which can befall the winemaker, explain them briefly and then move on. They rarely put them in to context with regard to their actual likelihood of occurrence. This leaves the newcomer, in particular, frightened and quite possibly over-fussy in his approach to the hobby. The truth is that the most prevalent disorder is a poor wine – it is as simple as that. It can be weak, insipid, bitter, over-sweet or plainly revolting. Sound recipes should not give such results very often, but if you insist upon producing large quantities of cheap "plonk" from liquidised tinned fruit alone you may end up with some pretty awful stuff. There are ways of making it palatable.

Insipid and "Thin" Wines
Avoidance should be obvious – construction of a sound, well-balanced recipe is the answer. However, experiments can go wrong and certainly the risk of a disappointment is inevitable in attempts to produce light, subtle and crisp dry wines.

Two bad habits which foster poor wines should be avoided. "Bonus" wines from making a second run on pulp which has been used once seem attractive on grounds of economy. If you do this, however, do not expect anything particularly drinkable. The second practice, which is not as common, is to refuse to throw away the lees after racking. These lees are poured into a spare demijohn under air-lock and gradually topped-up from the leftovers of other rackings. If you are lucky enough to avoid oxidisation, you might have a drinkable "slops wine" eventually, but the chances are that it will be very peculiar.

An insipid wine can be given a degree of character. It need not be consigned to the kitchen for casseroles yet. There are several ways in which you can add flavour. Obviously, you are not likely to be able to create an excellent wine because the deficiency will probably include body, which you cannot easily remedy. However, try one of the following:

Ginger   Suspend 3 or 4 ounces (about 100g) of root ginger (which has been broken with a nutcracker or light hammer) in the wine. The ginger is best placed in a muslin bag to keep escaping solids to a minimum. After 10 days or so a taste will indicate whether the strength of flavour is sufficient. If the wine is dry, add saccharine or other non-fermentable sweetener to taste. Even if you are not a particular fan of these sweeteners, the ginger will be powerful enough to mask any other flavour.

Citrus Fruit   Poor dry or sweet wines can be given a little interest by the use of the zest from either one grapefruit, two oranges or two lemons. Pare the zest carefully with an apple peeler or sharp knife, to avoid any white pith. Again, suspension in the wine in a muslin bag for about ten days will do the trick. In the old days the peel was placed in the oven to crisp before use, but the resultant flavour can be overpowering.

Proprietary Flavourings   Small bottles of concentrated flavourings are available in many types and you can try these if you wish. Be a little cautious in the quantity you use and pick your flavour with care.

Mulled Wine   Red wines, in particular, can be used for mulled wines if they are inferior. Save your poor wine for a party or a cold night and keep a box of Mulled Wine Sachets at hand. These can be purchased from health food shops or specialist winemakers' suppliers and they resemble miniature tea bags. Heat the wine in a saucepan, but do not allow it to boil. Suspend 2 or 3 bags of the herbs (per pint) in the wine while it heats. Before it reaches boiling point remove from the heat and add sugar to taste. Remove the herbs when the flavour is sufficient. It is surprising how guests will dispose of your reject wines when they have been treated in this way. If you have a slow crock-pot, this can be used to keep the mulled wine at the right temperature for those grateful visitors by switching it to the "low" setting.

Excessively Sweet Wines

Check your recipes to make sure that this outcome is unlikely and use a vigorous yeast. The area of greatest danger is in using modern convenience ingredients, where the sugar content is unpredictable. You can, of course, check the Original Gravity of your must before introducing the yeast. To do this, make up the must to about 9 pints (the extra is to allow for the pulp content) and take a reading with the hydrometer. An OG in excess of 1.100 might give you problems and an OG over 1.120 probably will – you can always dilute a little and discard the excess liquid. I have deliberately understated the sugar element in example recipes using tinned fruit in this book – it is better to have to add sugar towards the end of the fermentation than to be faced with an over-sweet wine.

If you suspect a stuck fermentation try the various remedies dealt with earlier. If your over-sweet wine is not to your liking go to the cupboard for some mulled wine sachets and throw another party.

But if the wine clearly has potential, do not despair. Place the demijohn on one side and make another gallon, this time using less sugar (reduce it by about 1 lb–450g). When the new wine has completed its pulp fermentation and has been sieved, mix the two and divide into two gallon jars. Each should ferment to dryness and you can feed with small amounts of sugar as necessary.

Occasionally you will not have exactly the same ingredients available for the second gallon, but all you need to find is a compatible ingredient which will blend successfully. There are sufficient mixed fruit recipes in Chapter 11 for you to find one. If not, make your second gallon from grape concentrate (again with a low sugar content) and combine this when the first, vigorous fermentation is complete.

Rumblings in the Cellar

If you meet a winemaker who has never had a cork blow out in his wine cupboard or cellar, you have met a remarkable man. Every now and then an apparently stable wine will decide to ferment on in the bottle. A good quality bottle will not normally shatter because the cork is the weak spot and it is here that the pressure will be evident. Keep an eye open for corks which start to squeeze forward out of the neck.

The reason for this problem will be either that you have bottled too early or that you have the phenomenon known as a malo-lactic ferment. The latter has been the subject of much investigation over the years, but let us just say here that the warmer weather of spring sometimes brings the bursting of more than just buds.

There is little excuse for bottling too early. Most likely you have decided that your fermentation has finished when it has merely stuck. It has become popular to try to stabilise at the bottling stage by the addition of a combination of sodium metabisulphite (as Campden tablets) and one of the two chemicals sold as "wine stabilisers". Many, however dislike sulphiting finished wine and stabilising tablets (or powder) are not foolproof.

If you do have a bottle blow, see a yeast deposit forming or notice a cork easing its way out, take great care in remedying the situation. You have a potential bomb. Remove the whole of the batch of the wine from your storage place at arm's length. Those corks which have started to move can usually be eased out by hand with the bottle pointed away from you, either over the sink or out of doors. Remove all of the corks in this way and pour the rescued wine into a clean demijohn. Allow it to ferment on to conclusion.

Persistent Hazes

Some wines refuse to clear. Finings, even filtering, fail to produce the star-bright results we require. Fortunately we have enzymes available to us which may assist and this is worth investigating.

Check the recipe notes. If it is fruit based, you may have pectin present. Try one or two teaspoons of pectolase, mixed thoroughly into the wine, and put it on one side for a few days.

If your recipe includes grain or vegetables (and there should not be many of these if you follow my advice) then you could have a starch haze. There is an enzyme available for this. Amylozyme 100 can be purchased readily and will break down the starch. As soon as your enzyme has had the desired effect rack the wine off the deposit.

Lack of tannin can also be a reason for failure to clear, so study your recipe and add $\frac{1}{4}$ teaspoon if you think that this could be the reason.

Should these treatments fail, the best remedy is likely to be time. Rather than bottling a hazy wine (which, if it does clear, will leave a nasty deposit in the bottle) store it in bulk. Buy a solid bung for your demijohn and put the gallon away for a few months to see if it drops clear naturally. The demijohn will not be suitable for bulk storage if there is a considerable air gap – the wine will almost certainly oxidise – so you will have to search for a smaller container if this is necessary.

Oxidisation

Neglect in allowing excessive air to be absorbed into the wine produces a distinctly unpleasant flavour. The most common cause is letting air-locks dry out during fermentation – keep them topped up. It is amazing how quickly the water in an air-lock will evaporate, particularly in high summer or if the jar is near a radiator.

Oxidisation cannot be totally avoided in the methods we use. Indeed, as has been stated already, we need a certain amount for the yeast. Every time you rack it will happen to some extent. Certainly when you filter there will be a degree of oxidisation.

It is the degree which matters. Careless, over-frequent racking (by splashing wine like a waterfall from one container to another) or leaving an excessive air-cushion at the top of the demijohn when the wine has stopped fermenting can give problems. Wines regularly recover from minor oxidisation; major oxidisation can impair them.

The most vulnerable time will be at pulp fermentation stage. If your yeast is slow to get going oxidisation can occur. This is one of the reasons why many winemakers sulphite before they begin. Others are confident enough in the yeast they use to proceed directly to the pulp fermentation with a well-prepared yeast starter.

Campden tablets are normally the recommended antidote for an oxidised wine, but sulphite in finished wines is not to everyone's taste. An alternative is to buy ascorbic acid (as vitamin C tablets) from your chemist and use ten or a dozen 100mg tablets per gallon. The problem here is that you will have increased the acidity and a further check and adjustment will be necessary.

Acetification

We are now coming to the real horrors which can befall us. They should not very often trouble the second stage winemaker.

Wine exposed to bacteria can become vinegar. The particular bacteria which, by stages, turns a good wine into acetic acid needs air to do its mischief and good winemaking practice will avoid this. A must which is in a bucket (however well covered) will be susceptible until it is fermenting well. Again the emphasis upon a good, well-started yeast, together with a warm position to encourage fermentation, cannot be overstated.

If you do get vinegar, throw it away and make a meticulous sterilisation of everything which could have come into contact with it.

Ropiness

This is caused by another bacteria which can attack light, white wines in particular. An average level of alcohol will normally give immunity but the same precautions at pulp fermentation stage are required. The wine takes on a viscous appearance as if it has a high glycerine content. If you can catch the bacteria early enough, a couple of Campden tablets may work, but advanced ropiness usually results in throwing the wine away and reaching for the sterilisation solution.

Flowers of Wine

Another horror, flowers of wine looks even more unpleasant. A film of mould gradually covers the surface. Again infection is airborne, but this time we have a yeast type. The same protective measures as used against acetification and ropiness apply. Throw affected wine away and sterilise well. The likelihood of this happening to an experienced or careful winemaker is very low.

CHAPTER 18

Final Touches

Only bottle your wine when you are perfectly happy with it – acidity, clarity and taste. Do not leave things to chance. Adjust the acidity level if necessary. Filter or fine if your wine does not sparkle and then test it on your palate. If there is anything wrong or not to your liking make the required adjustment or improvement referred to earlier.

Keep a range of sizes of bottle because it is inevitable that your wine (whether it is from one gallon fermenters or larger vessels) will not fill an exact number of standard wine bottles. A collection of 1 litre, 1½ litre and 2 litre bottles, some of which are clear for white wines and some of which are coloured for red wines, is very useful. Obviously you might have a bonus of a couple of glasses of young wine after you have bottled, however cleverly you mix your bottle sizes.

Very high quality commercial wines are not kept in bottles to mature, of course. The maturing of the wine takes place in wooden casks and here lies the essence of our problem in the wine cupboard. Ideally the wine needs to be able to breathe. It is generally accepted that the cork is not a sufficient means of providing the air which the wine really requires for its improvement during storage. On the other hand, few of us can afford wooden casks. There is a way of assisting the process, which we will come to later.

Fill your bottles to within ¼ inch to ½ inch (say 1cm) of the bottom of the cork. You can make a T-shaped piece of wood which rests in the neck of the bottle to show the correct fill or you can simply hold the cork, before fitting, against the side of the neck as a check that you have the right amount. Always lay corked bottles on their sides for storage.

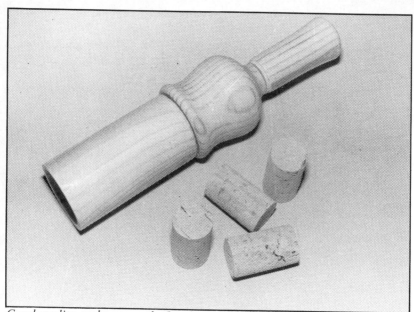

Good quality corks correctly fitted are essential for wine storage. A corker is not an expensive addition to the list of equipment used.

Rather than having a haphazard cupboard or cellar, divide it into three. A shelf or area marked "long-term", another marked "standard" and a third marked "quality" (or some other superlative) will serve a purpose. Obviously the long-term wines (such as heavy port-style or dry reds) can be in the least accessible areas, the everyday wines can be easy to reach. Any temptation which you or other members of the family might have to grab a bottle at random to go with Sunday lunch might be controlled in this way. Bear in mind in categorising your wines that white wines tend to mature more quickly than reds.

The shelf of the most promising "do not touch" wines should tempt you to try a little exhibiting, if you do not already do so. Join a wine circle or just enter a couple of bottles in your local flower and vegetable show – there is usually a class for both sweet and dry wines. Many of the recipes in this book are based upon proven winners.

It is at this point that two of the factors mentioned above come into play. Firstly, the larger than 70cl bottles are an advantage if

Another type of filter kit, using paper filters. Although most examples shown in this book bear Boots labels, a wide variety of equipment is sold at winemakers' shops.

you are going to show your best wines. You will, of course, want to check on the wine by tasting it and swirling it around in a glass to check for clarity while still having sufficient left to fill a sparkling clear exhibition bottle. You might also want to take second opinions of friends. Secondly, you might also wish to retain a litle surplus of the same to top up your winner when you sneak it back from the show and prepare to enter it in another class the following week!

More importantly, the show season gives you the ideal opportunity to assist in the maturing process. Wines do improve in bottles, whatever anyone tells you about the importance of wooden casks or barrels. But an annual injection of oxygen by way of a slight oxidisation will assist the improvement. When you are checking for show purposes make a point of emptying the bottle and pouring back gently before re-corking.

At this point you can also make certain that you do not have any hazes or deposits in the bottle. It is not uncommon for a wine which was "put down" in sparkling condition to throw a deposit

Some form of wine rack allowing horizontal storage is desirable and inexpensive ones are profuse. The heating tray shown is not essential except in cold room fermentation.

or develop a haze. The whole batch can be filtered and re-bottled if this has happened.

If you have a large output, do not bother with a fancy label on every bottle. You can label after you have selected the wine which you want to make public and have dusted it down. Expensive labels will only deteriorate in the cupboard. Using the recording method recommended earlier, all you need is a simple, sticky neck label:

B 29
BLACKBERRY
DRY

and you will have an instant check on its age (by the year code) and a reference number which will lead you to your recipe book for any other information.

Neck capsules look good but, in truth, the threat of infection through the corks if you do not use them is a fairly remote one.

Some plastic types are more economical, in that they can be removed intact (under running warm water), sterilised and used again. Your ordinary day to day wines can be kept without much risk.

Ideally your wine should be kept in the temperature range of 50–60°F and you can incorporate a thermostically controlled heater in your store cupboard for winter if you are a perfectionist or in search of trophies. Normally, however, a range of 40–70°F will not cause particular damage. One word of warning – avoid using your attic. It is tempting a fit a loft ladder and set up a range of bottle racks which are unlikely to be discovered by marauders. In high summer, however, most attics reach extremely high temperatures and you will almost certainly hear the muffled sound of explosions or see a trickle of red from a ceiling.

There is a great feeling of well-being and even prosperity available to the winemaker when he is able to survey a well-stocked cellar. Try to build up your reserves. Not only will it avoid the temptation to use excellent wines for ordinary occasions, but it will take the impatience out of your whole approach. It does not matter particularly how long a special new wine takes to ferment out if you have plenty of stocks to go at. Impatience is the bane of modern winemaking: it is the most disappointing aspect of the trends which have been apparent in recent years.

INDEX